S·T·R·O·K·E

Books by John H. Lavin

STROKE:
FROM CRISIS TO VICTORY

A HOSPITAL ADMINISTRATOR'S
GUIDE TO PURCHASING

S·T·R·O·K·E

FROM CRISIS TO VICTORY

A FAMILY
GUIDE

JOHN H. LAVIN

FRANKLIN WATTS
New York • Toronto
1985

Library of Congress Cataloging in Publication Data

Lavin, John H.
Stroke, from crisis to victory.

Includes index.
1. Cerebrovascular disease.   I. Title.   [DNLM:
1. Cerebrovascular Disorders—popular works.   WL 355 L412s]
RC388.5.L38   1985   616.8′1   84-26935
ISBN 0-531-09787-0

CONTENTS

ACKNOWLEDGMENTS

A book like this one owes much to many. I am deeply indebted to Amy and Andy Robertson and their four children, their friends, their relatives, and all who were personally associated with them during the ordeal described in these pages, including the private physicians who played a role in Andy's care. For reasons of family privacy, I have chosen not to identify them by their real names in the text, but all are real persons who willingly gave me their time so I could present to you one family's victory over stroke.

I must also thank the "strokers," as they often call themselves. Through stroke clubs in South Florida, I was able to communicate with and observe many of these stroke victors and their spouses. I found them uniformly inspiring, and I greatly appreciate the insights they gave me. This book may tell the story of one Florida stroke family, but there are thousands of such families throughout the country about whom it could have been written. I was fortunate to have the assistance of a number of them here.

In addition, I thank the many health professionals—the doctors, nurses, therapists, leaders of stroke clubs, agencies, and organizations—who made time for me in their busy schedules to discuss stroke in general and, where appropriate, to discuss Andy Robertson's case in particular. In the text I have used the real names of those engaged full-time in medical institutions or agencies active in stroke care, and I greatly appreciate their help. Their firsthand experiences led to much of the substance of this book.

The cooperation of these individuals was complemented by the cooperation of their agencies, associations, and institutions dealing with the problem of stroke. I particularly appreciate the help of the National Institute of Neurological and Communicative Disorders and Stroke; the American Heart Association and its Florida affiliate; Lee Memorial Hospital in Fort Myers, Florida; Morton F. Plant Hospital in Clearwater, Florida; the Veterans Administration Medical Center in Bay Pines, Florida; and many other medical institutions and agencies, including the Easter Seals Society of Dade County, Florida; the National Association of Rehabilitation Facilities; the National Center for Health Statistics; the National Stroke Association; Orlando, Florida Regional Hospital; and the University of Miami, Florida/ Jackson Memorial Medical Center. I am thankful for the use the American Heart Association let me make of material from its copyrighted publications *Aphasia and the Family* and *Stroke: Why Do They Behave That Way?* and for the use the NINCDS gave me of such publications as *The National Survey on Stroke* and *Guidelines for Stroke Care,* a handbook for health professionals.

Finally, I must thank my wife and my family and friends for the support they gave me during the difficult months of research and writing. My thanks also to Edna Partridge, who transcribed my interview tapes, and to my literary agent, Jean Naggar, and my editor, Ellen Joseph, for their roles in this project.

It was the confidence, assistance, and support of all of these combined that helped to produce *Stroke: A Family Guide from Crisis to Victory.*

JHL

This book is dedicated to my wife, Bernadette, for her patience, understanding, and love over the years, and to my four children, John S., Michael J., Eileen M., and Monica A., who have brought immeasurable joy to my life.

O · N · E

THE BEGINNING OF THE ORDEAL

We thought strokes only happened to older persons.

AMY ROBERTSON

When Andy Robertson awoke on the morning of January 31, 1977, he might easily have imagined for a moment that he was back in his native Michigan instead of living in southwestern Florida. Dark, winterish clouds covered the sun, a trace of rain chilled the air, promising more rain to come, and the temperature had fallen overnight into the low 40s.

Andy's wife, Amy, slept soundly in her twin bed beside him, and Andy was careful not to awaken her as he arose. Today was Amy's late day—she worked from noon to 9:00 p.m. at a department store five miles from home—and he knew she enjoyed the chance to linger in bed a bit later than usual on such mornings.

Andy could look at himself in the shaving mirror with some degree of pride this morning. True he was still overweight, a puffy 193 pounds on his 5-foot-9 frame, but he'd lost 24 pounds in the previous six months since his doctor had put him on a diet to get his blood pressure under control. His weight battle was a constant one—he'd been up to 230 pounds a few years earlier—but he was winning it. And his blood pressure, with the aid of medication, had come down to normal for a forty-seven-year-old man.

Once out of his bedroom, Andy had less need to move quietly. Three of their four children lived at home but were already up and out of the house. Sally, nineteen, started her workday at 7:00 a.m., and Susie, seventeen, a high school senior, had already rumbled off in her pickup truck to morning classes, the truck a working vehicle for a girl very active in the Future Farmers of America. Doug, at twenty-five, oldest of the Robertson children, was ambitiously working two jobs, launching a career in real estate sales and driving a truck for a construction firm for needed income. With younger son Donald, a twenty-four-year-old Army veteran, living at college in a nearby city, Andy had the freedom of an empty house—except, of course, for Duke, an affectionate gray poodle who followed playfully as Andy prepared for work. It was a freedom Andy would reluctantly have to get used to in the years to come, but he had no warning of that now.

By 8:30 or so, dressed meticulously as usual, his thinning brown hair groomed carefully, his rimmed glasses giving a studious look to his oval face, he sat down to his light breakfast, a pleasant-looking man who could pass easily for a school principal or an insurance salesman. Actually, Andy had recently started his new career in real estate.

Some eight years earlier, Andy and Amy had been glad to move to Florida from a suburban neighborhood in Detroit. Andy had been in the family lumber business there with his father and brother, but, after twenty years, when his father had indicated he was ready to retire to Florida, the younger Robertsons were eager for the change, too. In fact, Amy's parents—who were living in Massachusetts, where she had met Andy when he was

— 3 —

a naval flight attendant—were also ready to extend their Florida vacations to permanent residence.

So a family migration began. The older couples moved down first, Andy and Amy staying north to await the construction of their new house while Andy oversaw the sale of the lumberyard and the dissolution of the business. He and young Doug even drove a truckload of paneling, molding, and other special lumber south for the new house in the interim.

Amy was delighted when the time came to leave her small house in Michigan and move into her large, attractive new home just a few miles from Andy's parents and her own. While Andy was outgoing and affable, Amy, a slim, attractive, dark-haired woman of forty-five, was quiet and reserved, "a sweet lady who would do anything for her husband," as one friend describes her. Although she worked, she was what might be called a traditional homemaker whose interests centered largely on her husband and children, content in the role of housewife caring for the home and family. Her new home would be something to look after—five bedrooms, one for each of the four children as well as the master bedroom, three and a half baths, a family room, a living room, a kitchen with all the expected modern appliances, a swimming pool and surrounding screened patio, or lanai, just off the living room, even the prerequisite palm trees outside their one-story Spanish-style building. The house was just off the corner in an attractive, well-kept suburban development of similar homes that sold, in those days of the late 1960s, for about $40,000 to $60,000. Today they command $150,000 to $175,000 and more.

House and furniture were paid for in full when the family settled in to live. That was fortunate because financial affairs did not go well for the Andy Robertsons after the move south. Andy's and his partner's new business venture in the restaurant equipment field soured quickly, though it dragged on for four or five years before collapsing completely, severely depleting family resources. Then Andy turned to a Florida business staple, real estate, getting his sales license and going to work for a major developer. But that was just in time for the 1973–74 recession, and sales were very slow.

In 1973, Amy went to work, selling men's clothing at a department store. It was to be just a temporary measure to pay for extras like lunch out at a nice restaurant or new clothes. But as Andy's business struggles continued, her income became increasingly important to the family. It became even more important when the Robertsons had to take out a $25,000 mortgage on the house to meet other debt requirements. Still, Amy says, the family was managing to live comfortably, if somewhat more conservatively, at home.

A break came in October 1976, when Andy passed a test to become a licensed real estate broker and moved a step up in his new field. After one brief—but costly—false start, he was invited to join an old associate in a local real estate firm. By this dreary Monday morning, the last day of January, both Andy and Amy saw the beginnings of a change in fortune. Andy was not yet producing income, but Amy's earnings were tiding them over and prospects looked as bright as they had always expected them to be. "We always thought the future would be great," Amy says.

Andy was not dwelling on his considerable financial pressures this January morning. A naturally good-humored man, his spirits were high despite the dreariness of the weather outside. His cousin and friend, Jim Murphy, who had been employed in the family lumber business before starting a business of his own, was flying his own plane down from Michigan on business still farther south in Florida. Whenever Jim flew down, he phoned Andy in advance and then stopped off at the Clearwater–St. Petersburg airport, where the two of them would get together. Andy was to meet him there for lunch today.

Jim Murphy remembers that January 31 well. The skies were clear when he got to the small airport in Michigan. They had to be or he couldn't have taken off; he wasn't licensed to fly in bad weather. Departing about 7:00 a.m. from about 40 miles west of Detroit, he made his refueling stop in Knoxville, Tennessee, and then headed for Florida. He'd arrive there about 1:00, and he was looking forward to it; he always enjoyed getting together with Andy and swapping stories about family, friends, and business, talking, as he puts it, about all the things old friends talk about when they get together.

They met on schedule, had a Scotch and soda, and chatted amiably over lunch. "Even when things were bad, as they were then," Murphy says of Andy, "he was happy. He had a wonderful sense of humor." The time slipped pleasantly by, and, too soon for a couple of old friends, Jim Murphy had to leave. Andy walked with him out to the small plane. A brief rain shower had passed, and the skies were clearing. Andy watched Jim take off, followed the small plane southward with his eyes until it disappeared, then walked back to his car. He remembers getting in. He remembers starting the car. He remembers driving away from the airport. He remembers nothing else of that day or, for that matter, of the next several weeks. Nor did Jim Murphy know as he soared away that his forty-seven-year-old cousin was about to become a victim of the nation's third most deadly menace—stroke.

Others remember more of that day. Amy returned from work about 9:30 p.m. Sally and Susie were sitting on the floor in the living room, watching a special on television. Doug had gone out for the evening. Andy was standing over the girls, looking down at them, his hands in his pockets. He said nothing, didn't even greet Amy when she came in. "I thought he must be angry about something," Amy says. "I tried to think of what I might have done to make him angry, but I couldn't think of anything."

Or was Andy teasing, as he often did? Several times he spoke to the girls, but his words came out thick and indecipherable. "He stuttered," Sally says. He also walked away from them, walked aimlessly out of the room, back in, over to the girls again. Amy had gone into the kitchen to prepare her late supper.

"Mom," Sally called to her, "will you get him out of here. He's bugging us."

"Andy," Amy called in, "leave the girls alone." Suddenly, for the first time since she'd come home, he spoke to her. "I want pido," he said.

Amy looked at him incredulously. "Pido?" she said.

"Pido," he insisted emphatically. "I want pido."

Still unsure whether Andy was in one of his usual joking moods or was angry, Amy replied with mock anger: "OK," she said, "I'll go get your pido!"

She walked into their bedroom, brought Andy's pillow back with her, and, in keeping with the game, thrust it at him. "Here, here's your pido."

Andy showed her a satisfied smile, took the pillow in his arms, walked into his bedroom, undressed, and went to bed. The rest of the family went back to watching television.

Andy remembers none of this, nor was he aware the following morning, Tuesday, February 1, that the weather turned sunny. The temperature climbed from an overnight low of 35 into the high 50s. It was Amy's day off, a day on which she usually caught up with her housework, a beautiful day in southwest Florida. Andy was sleeping late.

"He'd always been in the sort of business where he'd been his own boss," Amy says, "and every once in a while he would stay in bed all morning. So I thought, well, this is another one of those mornings, and I'll let him sleep."

Marv Chester, however, Andy's associate in Chester's real estate firm, was watching the clock and growing concerned. "We were having an office meeting here about 8:30 that morning," Chester says, "and Andy was always one of the very first to be at such meetings." He started to telephone Andy's home, but something interrupted and the phone call didn't get made. Chester made a mental note to call Andy later that day.

Meanwhile, as the morning wore on, Amy was also becoming concerned. She'd slip quietly into the bedroom and look at Andy lying there. He seemed to be sleeping peacefully, his breathing quite normal. She began to check on him more frequently, to make less effort to be quiet, to make sure he was breathing. By afternoon she was convinced that his sleep was somehow unnatural. Older son Doug came home about that time.

"I think something's wrong with Daddy," Amy told him. "He hasn't gotten up yet."

They talked it over, tried unsuccessfully to rouse Andy, then called the family doctor, George Romson, whose office was in Clearwater. As Amy spoke to the doctor on the phone, Doug beside her, they suddenly heard Andy in the bedroom. He was crying.

From Amy's account over the phone and his own knowledge of Andy's health, Romson immediately recognized the symptoms. "It sounds like a stroke," Amy remembers him saying. "Better get him to the hospital right away."

Stroke. Two physicians, one of them Romson, had raised a warning of that to Andy in the preceding months. "But it didn't sink in," Amy says. "He felt well, and he was so young. That was the main thing, he was so young. He thought strokes happened to older people, and so did I. My grandmother had one, and his aunt had one and spent five years in a nursing home. But she was older too. It didn't mean much to us."

Now, dramatically, it did. Doug pulled up his car on the lawn, right to the front door, and telephoned a friend, Todd, who raced over from his nearby business to provide assistance. Amy stayed with Andy. He opened his eyes, but he couldn't speak. She noticed that he would move his left arm and leg but there was no movement on his right side. Fear and guilt gripped her, fear at what had happened to Andy, guilt for not having called the doctor sooner. (The doctors say an earlier call probably wouldn't have made any difference in Andy's case.)

Doug and Todd managed to hoist Andy erect from the bed, draping his arms over their shoulders as much as possible and providing his support. He put a little weight on his left leg, none on his right. As they half-carried, half-dragged him to the front door, he began crying again, tears streaming down his face.

That was the scene Sally walked in on as she returned home from work. Amy hurriedly explained what was happening, but the shock of seeing her helpless father in tears was too much for Sally to accept all at once. She burst into tears and ran into the bathroom. Amy remembers leaving her there alone, crying.

Carefully and with great effort, the boys got Andy into the front seat of Doug's car on the passenger side. Amy isn't sure yet why she didn't call an ambulance. Maybe she didn't think of it; maybe she thought about the cost and their financial problems. She climbed into the back seat directly behind Andy and put her arms around him, holding him tightly against the seat.

Doug got behind the wheel, and they set off on a nightmarish twenty-minute ride, Amy straining throughout to keep Andy from falling forward or sideways, Doug weaving through heavy, late afternoon traffic of home-bound cars. Amy felt her first seconds of relief as she saw large Morton Plant Hospital looming ahead of them. Just as they pulled up to the emergency room entrance, Andy began to throw up in the car.

Things happened very swiftly after that. Attendants rushed to the car, removed Andy and placed him on a gurney, and whisked him into the hospital. Amy and Doug suddenly found themselves sitting in the waiting room outside the emergency room, their hearts still racing, nothing to do now but wait. Amy telephoned Donald at college and told him what the doctor had said. Donald told her he'd leave for the hospital immediately. Later she telephoned the store where she worked to explain what had happened and told her employer: "I don't know when I'll be back." The employer was understanding, sympathetic.

Donald arrived at the emergency room and joined his mother and brother. Amy had made up her mind she wouldn't cry. Andy is going to be OK, she told herself. "I thought, 'It will take him a year to recover, but we're in no hurry. We'll just take one day at a time, and in a year he'll be fine.'"

T · W · O

WHAT
IS A
STROKE?

*Stroke is usually the culmination
of progressive disease that may
extend over many years and that
is not always detectable in a
routine physical examination.
In many cases there are no warning
signs, and, thus, the stroke is a
particularly terrifying event.*

NATIONAL INSTITUTE OF NEUROLOGICAL AND
COMMUNICATIVE DISORDERS AND STROKE

There was far less optimism in the emergency room of Morton Plant Hospital that first day of February 1977 when Andy Robertson was wheeled in about 4:00 p.m. His condition was considered grave.

Dr. Romson was there waiting with the ER (emergency room) staff. They examined Andy immediately. His skin was warm and moist. His lungs and throat were clear, his heart beating regularly at a normal rate. There was no stiffness in his neck, indicating that his stroke was more likely caused by a blockage or a constriction of a cerebral artery than by a hemorrhage in the brain. At first they found rigid paralysis of his right arm and leg, overactive reflexes, and a blood pressure that had soared to 190 over 100. Because he had vomited, they inserted a tube into his nose and passed it down into his stomach to remove its contents, keep his airway clear, and prevent respiratory problems, including aspiration pneumonia—the clogging of the respiratory system with food particles. A spinal tap was done, and no blood was found in his cerebrospinal fluid, another indication that the stroke had not been hemorrhagic. His eyes were shifted to the left and fixed. The right side of his face was paralyzed.

The rigid paralysis on his right side soon gave way to a flaccid paralysis, his right limbs just lying there loosely, unmoving, his reflexes now failing to respond. He appeared to have some sensation on his right side—but very little—in response to a pin prick or touch.

He was unable to speak, had some—but little—response to attempts to rouse him. When doctors moved a finger in front of his face, Andy would try to follow it with his eyes. He would open his mouth on command but was unable to respond to a command to stick out his tongue. Romson put a finger into Andy's left hand and told him to squeeze. He squeezed. Into his right hand. No response.

A catheter was inserted to withdraw his urine, and an IV was started to maintain his fluid balance. He was given medication to reduce edema— the swelling of his brain. Such swelling can cause the death of additional cells. Because of his age and the seriousness of his condition, an extensive neurological and medical work-up was ordered, and a neurologist, Bradley Jackson, was called in. A nuclear brain scan was done to rule out a brain tumor and other possible alternatives to stroke. Later a CAT (computerized axial tomography) scan would show massive infarction—death of brain tissues—and evidence of brain swelling.

Andy was diagnosed as having suffered a cerebrovascular occlusion, the closing off—almost certainly by a clot—of his left middle cerebral artery, blocking the flow of blood to the left side of his brain and causing massive death of brain tissue.

The type of stroke and the location of the damaged artery in the brain are major factors that determine the type and extent of the damage a stroke causes. Different arteries feed different brain cells, which, in turn, control specific functions of the brain and body. A blocked artery that causes the death of brain tissue in the left side, or left hemisphere, of the brain—as Andy's did—results in disabilities to the right side of the body. Damage to the right hemisphere or right half of the brain affects the left side of the body. **Only in a small percentage of stroke cases is there resultant disability to both sides of the body.**

You will hear stroke referred to by any number of names—apoplexy, cerebrovascular accident or CVA, ruptured aneurysm, cerebral hemorrhage, ischemic attack, cerebral infarction, and more. Whatever it's called, **stroke,** as Andy's case illustrates, **is a sudden, often severe disability of the body brought on by a disruption in the supply of blood to the brain.** The underlying factor in all strokes is simply this: **Stroke occurs when the blood fails to get through to some of the brain cells with their needed supply of oxygen.**

Many strokes are fatal; most are not. Most leave some permanent residual damage; a small percentage leave no permanent damage at all.

Think of Andy Robertson's blood as a freight train moving through a tunnel called a cerebral artery. As he laughed and joked at lunch with his cousin that previous day, a blockage in that tunnel was about to cut off the train's constant supply of nutrients and oxygen vitally needed by his delicate brain cells or nerves. That supply must not be interrupted even for a few minutes. Suddenly it was. The supply train was halted. In a minute, two, four, ten, brain cells beyond that point began to die from lack of oxygen. The greater the area of the brain cut off from this blood-oxygen supply, the greater the "infarction" or death of brain tissues.

What his doctors had to determine initially was whether the blood-train had been blocked by a clogged or constricted artery or whether it had burst through the tunnel wall, spilling blood into the brain or into the area surrounding the brain. In that case, the blood would not only fail to reach the cells for oxygen delivery, but the weight of the spilled blood would have put such pressure on cells it covered that many of them, too, would die.

Diagnosis differentiates between two broad classifications of stroke— ischemic and hemorrhagic. Any stroke you have observed must fall into one of these two categories. The nation's most comprehensive and far-reaching study on stroke to date, the National Survey on Stroke conducted by the National Institute of Neurological and Communicative Disorders and Stroke, defines each type as follows:

Ischemic stroke, the type Andy suffered, is the result of a reduction of blood flow through an artery in the brain or neck, due either to a blockage or a constriction, thereby depriving brain cells of needed oxygen and causing "infarction," or cell death. This type of stroke is also referred to as an infarction stroke or an ischemic infarction.

Hemorrhagic stroke is caused by the breaking of a cerebral blood vessel and the subsequent spilling of blood into the brain tissue or its surrounding area.

Note that both types of stroke are the *result* of a blood circulation problem in the brain, not the cause of a constricted, blocked, or burst artery.

When Andy Robertson suffered his ischemic stroke, the death of or injury to cells in the left hemisphere of his brain meant that that portion of the brain could no longer get its messages or orders heard or understood by other parts of his brain or body. Some of those injured cells could be expected to recover. Meanwhile, in any stroke patient, paralysis of an upper and lower limb, or its milder cousin, paresis (slight or partial paralysis), may occur. Speech, memory, movement, all may be affected, mildly, moderately, or severely, temporarily or permanently. It is this very difference in the degree of permanent damage and the extent of possible recovery in just a matter of months, regardless of how severe the initial effects of the stroke appear to be, that should bolster the hopes and the efforts of stroke victims and their families, especially in those difficult immediate days and weeks after the attack. Amy Robertson's optimism came from within, but never forget that most stroke victims do become stroke victors and that two factors are paramount to their recovery: their own motivation and their family's support.

There is a good deal more that families like the Robertsons can learn about specific types of stroke and their effects in order to be able to respond better to a stroke victim's needs. Ischemic strokes come in two principal types: thrombotic and embolic. Don't let those medical terms frighten you; they both mean clots in the blood that can close off a cerebral artery. The difference between them lies in where the clot originates.

Thrombotic infarction. If the clot originates in a cerebral artery or in a carotid artery of the neck, where it is generally associated with a buildup of a fatty substance called plaque along the artery's interior walls, narrowing the tunnel the blood must pass through, the clot is called a thrombus and the stroke is a thrombotic infarction.

Embolic infarction. If the clot forms away from the brain, say in the heart, it is called an embolus. A piece of the clot breaks loose and is carried along by the blood through the vessels. As it reaches the brain, where the arteries become smaller and smaller to serve minute areas of cells, the clot reaches a point at which it can proceed no farther. It plugs the vessel like a cork in a bottle, cutting off the blood supply. That sudden blockage is called an embolism, and the stroke is an embolic infarction.

The hemorrhage category also includes two major types of stroke. Generally, a **cerebral hemorrhage**—the bursting of a blood vessel in the brain— occurs when the blood, flowing past a weak section in the wall of an artery, causes the artery to bulge out or balloon at that point. This balloon, or sac, is called an **aneurysm**. Eventually, from the constant pressure of the blood swelling its size and the continued weakening of its walls, the balloon is likely to burst—or, in clinical terms, the cerebral aneurysm ruptures.

A **parenchymatous hemorrhage**, or **intraparenchymatous hemorrhage (IPH)**, occurs when the blood flows through that opening in the tunnel wall into the brain tissue. The term "parenchymatous" (pronounced par-eng-kim-ah-tus) simply refers to an essential part of an organ, in this case brain tissue.

A **subarachnoid hemorrhage (SAH)** occurs when the blood flows instead from the ruptured artery into the space surrounding the brain, which is called the subarachnoid (sub-ah-rak-noid) space.

Thrombosis is the cause of the great majority of strokes. The National Survey identifies it in more than 80 percent of the almost two thousand strokes studied, with each of the other three types accounting for approximately 6 percent or so apiece. Other studies put the rates of occurrence at about 80 percent for thrombotic strokes, 5 percent for embolic strokes, and 15 percent for the two types of hemorrhagic stroke combined. The hemorrhagic strokes are more common in younger persons—actress Patricia Neal, for instance, had a hemorrhagic stroke at age thirty-eight—and the hemorrhagic strokes are more often fatal. Overall, only 40 percent of patients survive hemorrhagic strokes, while 75 percent survive strokes involving arterial blockage. If the hemorrhage is massive or is in the brain stem, death may occur within a few hours or days.

Working in Andy Robertson's favor that day was the fact that survival is partly dependent on the age of the victim and on the type of stroke. Younger patients with nonhemorrhagic strokes survive best. And, by stroke standards, that meant Andy.

His attack indicates another important fact about stroke: **Although we tend to think of stroke as a sudden, swift, lightning-like strike, a stroke may take hours to run its course. Strokes come with a variety of symptoms. Among the most common are impaired consciousness, stupor, and coma, with the victim's state of consciousness generally fluctuating. Other symptoms, most of them more common when bleeding strokes are involved, include headache, stiff neck, vertigo, seizures and convulsions, nausea and vomiting, tingling, and abnormal vision, including double vision.**

Researchers have found that signs and symptoms may be slow to appear when the bleeding is into the space around the brain. In fact, judging by the National Survey of hospitalized patients, almost 10 percent of persons suffering such strokes aren't admitted to the hospital for a week or more after the hemorrhage occurs. In contrast, if the bleeding is directly into the brain tissue, the stroke victim tends to be taken to the hospital within a day of the attack. On average among those hospitalized, patients, like Andy

Robertson, who suffer blood-flow blockages are admitted later than hemorrhagic patients. So Amy Robertson's delay the morning that Andy remained in bed was far from exceptional. Most of the stroke patients studied, almost 85 percent, were hospitalized within three days of onset.

Thus, patients arrive at a hospital with strokes in one of two stages. Either they have a **progressive stroke**, also called a stroke in evolution, in which the lack of oxygen has been present in the brain for hours or more and in which the patient's condition is continuing to deteriorate; or, as in Andy's case, they have a **completed stroke**, in which the maximum damage has been done and the patient's condition has stabilized.

Many of the effects of stroke that Andy showed evidence of in the emergency room that day, like stroke's symptoms, are common to stroke in general. For instance, more than half of all stroke patients suffer hemiplegia—the paralysis that affected one side of Andy's body—or hemiparesis, partial paralysis of one side. This disability occurs slightly more often in ischemic than in hemorrhagic strokes.

Andy's inability to speak as a result of his stroke is another common effect. In fact, it puts him among the almost 75 percent of "right hemiplegics" who suffer speech disorders. Such disorders affect almost 60 percent of "left hemiplegics" as well. Aphasia—loss of speech or understanding—is almost twice as common in right hemiplegics as in left hemiplegics, but dysphasia—speech impairment—and dysarthria—poor articulation—occur about equally in ischemic strokes of either side. Facial paralysis or weakness is more common in ischemic strokes.

We will look in much greater detail in a later chapter at the damage and the effects that occur based on which side of the brain is affected. For now it is enough to understand that there are distinct mental and physical changes that may occur after stroke, depending on which side of the brain is damaged.

Diagnosing the type of stroke that Andy suffered was a primary consideration of the emergency room team because the differences among the four major types can be crucial to both treatment and recovery. Nevertheless, and despite all that is known about stroke, arriving at an accurate diagnosis can be extremely difficult for doctors simply because it requires them, in effect, to look into the patient's brain. A mistake can be life-threatening. Suppose, for instance, doctors diagnosed a stroke as ischemic and it was actually hemorrhagic? If they had prescribed a "blood thinner" to try to facilitate the flow of blood through a blocked artery, they instead could actually have been speeding the flow of blood through a ruptured artery into the brain or surrounding area, making matters far worse.

Fortunately, diagnostic equipment keeps improving. To the CAT scans of Andy's experience have been added new scanning techniques—positron emission tomography (PET) and nuclear magnetic resonance (NMR)—that allow a physician to examine the brain as never before. With ultrasound, surgeons can now detect clots deep within the brain, and, in one ultrasound experiment, they have been able to detect atherosclerosis in a carotid, or neck, artery. As the expensive equipment involved in these processes becomes more widely available in hospitals, diagnoses should be surer. Meanwhile, the more standard tests in use include the spinal tap, such as Andy received, to check for blood in the cerebrospinal fluid, electroencephalogram, or brain wave examination, isotopic brain scans, and angiography.

All of these factors were almost automatically being taken into consideration by the medical team that worked over Andy Robertson that February evening as, just steps away on the other side of the emergency room walls, Amy and her sons waited. At 6:30, their wait was over. Andy was rolled out of emergency and into an elevator that would take him up to the sixth floor neurological intensive care unit (NICU). Dr. Romson stayed below and sought out the Robertsons, who formed closely around him. Andy's condition was still guarded, he told them, but his blood pressure had come down quickly to 160 over 100 and then to a more satisfactory 140 over 80. That raised the question of whether high blood pressure had triggered the stroke or whether Andy's realization that something was wrong with him had elevated his blood pressure. It was a question without an answer.

Then Romson gave them the news they'd been hoping for: They could see Andy in the ICU, but just briefly. They were directed to the elevator and the unit. The nurses and other staff at the emergency room were particularly kind to them. Even as the elevator lights flashed the numbers of the passing floors, Amy had difficulty believing what had happened. Andy was so young, she kept thinking. But she knew, too, that he had a medical history and some specific warnings associated with stroke. It was easy to remember them now.

T · H · R · E · E

PROGRAMMED FOR A STROKE

*He had hypertension,
was overweight, smoked, and in
general lived the kind of life that
contributed to his disease.*

NEUROLOGIST DR. BRADLEY JACKSON

H ospital elevators seem to move very slowly as they take an anxious spouse or family member to the bedside of a critically ill loved one. They stop at floors where no one is waiting to get on and no one gets off. Elevator doors stay open at each stop long enough to prompt fretful passengers to press heavily on the buttons for their floors again and again. Other passengers who do get on or off seem to take interminably long about it. Amy and her sons felt the pressures of such a ride. She was still struggling to accept the fact that her husband of twenty-six years was somewhere on a floor above, a stroke victim barely holding on to life. "Why Andy?" she thought, as the elevator slowly carried her upward. "Why has this happened to him?" Still, she knew that the warning signs had been there. Two doctors had pointed them out.

What are **the warning signs of stroke**? Some are sudden and are indicative of immediate danger. Others exist long-term, are sometimes genetic, sometimes attributable to lifestyle. The American Heart Association lists seven warning signs of stroke, which, with the Association's copyright permission, follow:

1. A sudden or temporary weakness or numbness of the face, arm, or leg.

2. Temporary difficulty with or loss of speech or trouble understanding speech.

3. Sudden, temporary dimness or loss of vision, particularly in one eye.

4. An episode of double vision.

5. Unexplained headaches or a change in the pattern of one's headaches.

6. Temporary dizziness or unsteadiness.

7. A recent change in personality or mental ability.

In July 1976, seven months before his stroke, Andy experienced warning sign number 3. Suddenly, the vision in his left eye faded down to a pinhole. It stayed that way briefly, then returned to normal. It scared him—but he didn't know then that it was related to stroke. He called an eye doctor in Clearwater and made an immediate appointment.

That was July 1. The eye doctor, William Clawson, remembers their encounter. For four minutes that morning, Andy told him, the vision from his left eye was that of a man looking out of a narrow tunnel. Three days earlier, he'd had a sharp pain in that eye and a dull throbbing at the back of his head on the left side. Maybe, he thought, he needed a change in eyeglasses.

Clawson took a medical history and checked Andy's vision. Andy told him his health had been good but that he'd been on diet pills. Maybe they were a factor, he said. His vision was normal now, and he felt well. No, he said in answer to Clawson's question, he didn't have hypertension.

Hypertension—high blood pressure, as it is also called—is at the top of everyone's list of factors that can cause stroke. As the National Survey on Stroke put it: "A history of elevated blood pressure was present in approximately 60 percent of patients with either subarachnoid hemorrhage or thrombotic infarction, in about 70 percent with intraparenchymal hemorrhage, and in about 40 percent of embolic infarctions." In addition, *Guidelines for Stroke Care*, a government-published syllabus for doctors and other health professionals, reports that persons with hypertension will have two to four times more strokes than those without hypertension.

Both Andy and his father had high blood pressure. In fact, back in March 1970, Romson had examined Andy and found his weight at 228 pounds, his blood pressure at 150 over 100. Romson took the first step doctors would generally take. Since hypertension is associated with obesity, he advised Andy to get his blood pressure under control by losing weight. Three months later, when Romson checked Andy, the blood pressure was down to 138 over 90, but Andy had lost only three pounds. Not enough, Romson fussed at him; he had to stick more closely to his diet. By April 1972, Andy had lost 40 pounds, weighed 190, and had a blood pressure reading that was normal for him at 132 over 80. But his battle with the diet was almost constant. By November 1973, he'd put on 5 pounds, though his blood pressure had stayed down, 136 over 88. He could cheerfully tell Romson that he was walking several miles a day then and exercising.

Undoubtedly, by the time of his visit to Clawson, Andy really felt that his hypertension was behind him. But Clawson found Andy's blood pressure to be 160 over 100. An examination of Andy's eyes showed evidence of arteriosclerosis, which established the potential for certain blood vessels in the retina of the eye to close or spasm. There was also some normal thickening of the blood vessel walls of the retina that comes with aging.

Clawson told Andy this was not a time to be concerned about eyeglasses. It was a time to be concerned about something potentially far more serious. "My impression was that he had had a vascular spasm without any specific eye problem at the time," the doctor says, "and that he had hypertension and arteriosclerosis. I told him I was concerned about further occlusive disease that could give rise to something like a stroke." Clawson advised Andy to call his family doctor.

"I was concerned about the potential danger to him," the eye doctor

— 20 —

recalls. "Not everyone with hypertension or the normal arteriosclerotic changes of aging is a stroke candidate," he notes. "It's a combination of disease, control of the disease, and unexplained visual loss or temporary interruption of vision that can wave the red flag." Then, he adds, the problem can be vascular, not visual.

What Andy had suffered is also called a focal transient ischemic attack, or TIA. The clinical name "transient ischemic" simply translates to "temporary deficiency" of blood flowing to the brain cells or, as in Andy's case, possibly to the retina of the eye. The oxygen supply is disturbed only briefly, and recovery is usually complete and within twenty-four hours. TIAs are often called "little strokes" and are frequently regarded as warnings of more devastating strokes. As was borne out in Andy's case, **the risk of further stroke is highest in the first year after the initial attack**, according to the government-published *Guidelines*, and about 35 percent of TIA victims are likely to suffer another stroke within five years of their transient experience.

Two other types of stroke are somewhat similar to TIAs. Reversible ischemic neurological deficits, or RINDs, are different only in that the temporary effect of a RIND may last a week or two. Arteriosclerotic dementia, which comprises only a very small percentage of cases, is a form of stroke in which patients suffer recurrent attacks that leave them mentally impaired.

Other factors were also working against Andy, such as stress. **Although a direct one-to-one relationship between stress and stroke has not yet been established,** physicians are quick to point out that, as Dr. Romson puts it, **"Stress can raise the blood pressure, and intense stress can raise it markedly."** Those associated with Andy at the time of his stroke agree that he was under intense financial stress.

Stress may also cause a weakening of the body's defenses overall, a concept that is now only in the exploratory stage. But many researchers agree that a lessening of stress or the conversion of abnormal stress to normal stress may indirectly help the stroke-prone person.

Diet, lack of exercise, and other factors can be associated with stroke in general and with Andy Robertson's stroke in particular with a greater or lesser degree of certainty. Some research shows that elevated serum cholesterol in persons under age fifty moderately increases the risk of ischemic stroke. Many doctors say diets high in cholesterol and triglycerides help form the fatty tissue that thickens the artery walls, narrows the tunnel, and may close it entirely by thrombotic attack. During one of Andy's earlier physical examinations, both his cholesterol and his triglycerides had been found to be elevated, indicative of too much fat in his vascular system, fat that could eventually interrupt the flow of blood through an artery.

Andy was also basically a sedentary person, like so many office workers, and sedentary persons who eschew exercise are felt to have a higher risk of heart problems. These problems, in turn, are associated with a higher risk of stroke.

Although Andy had shown no evidence of heart disease himself, **heart disease has been found to be two to three times as frequent in patients who have had strokes as in a similar population who have not had strokes.** Overall, the National Survey found that about 60 percent of some 1,600 stroke patients studied had some type of heart disease.

As might be expected, there is a higher risk of embolic strokes—those caused by the breaking away of a piece of blood clot from the heart area or another area away from the brain and its subsequent clogging of a brain artery. Among patients studied who had embolic strokes, 8 percent had a history of heart attack and 35 percent had a history of valvular heart disease.

Other chronic heart diseases, especially those associated with atherosclerosis—the buildup of plaque in the arteries—were found in almost 60 percent of stroke patients; the exception to that was the subarachnoid hemorrhage patients, where the finding was just under 25 percent. As the *Guidelines* put it, if atherosclerosis is found in other parts of the body, its presence can be suspected in the cerebral arteries as well. **In fact, the National Heart, Lung, and Blood Institute notes that the major risk factors of stroke are so similar to those for heart attacks that activities concerned with preventing one of those disorders should help prevent the other.**

Although what constitutes high blood pressure varies with each individual and with age, hypertension, which has no known cause, can nevertheless be controlled by diet, lifestyle, and, if necessary, medication prescribed by a physician. Not only is it treatable but, in the hope of preventing stroke, the *Guidelines* recommend permanent antihypertensive therapy, when tolerated, for all ages if elevated blood pressure is found. Depending on the severity of the hypertension, the medication is often the therapy of second choice. The Joint National Committee on the Detection, Evaluation, and Treatment of High Blood Pressure advises those with hypertension to help themselves by keeping their intakes of alcohol and salt low and their weight down, by reducing their blood cholesterol by reducing fats in their diet, and by exercising. Cigarette smoking, associated with the risk of heart disease, is therefore at least a secondary risk factor for stroke and should be stopped. New findings continue to augment stroke-prevention tactics. Recent clinical studies, for instance, indicate that aspirin may lower the incidence of subsequent stroke among TIA victims. But like any other therapy, aspirin therapy should be carried out only under the guidance and approval of a physician.

Though Andy's list of stroke risks was great, it did not include one of the more common contributory factors, diabetes. **Researchers cannot fully explain why diabetes is a factor in stroke, but they agree that it is.** The

National Survey found that 22 percent of all stroke patients had a history of diabetes, against a comparable 7 percent in the general population. One long-term study indicates that any impairment in glucose tolerance, such as in diabetes, raises the risk of cerebrovascular accident. Physicians note also that diabetics have vascular diseases—and usually thrombotic strokes. On the other hand, because diabetes causes blood vessel problems throughout the body and therefore can lead to heart attacks, it is a factor in embolic strokes as well. Again, control of diabetes on an individual basis can reduce the risk of stroke.

Several other factors have been cited as possibly contributing to the risk of stroke. Anemia is one, and a sudden or prolonged fall in blood pressure is another. A noise in a carotid artery in the neck may indicate a stenosis—a narrowing of the tunnel inside the artery—which may be a sign of impending stroke. Many reports indicate that there is a significantly higher occurrence of stroke among young women who take oral contraceptives than in a similar group of young women who do not. And finally, although the data are inconclusive, several studies indicate that a history of cerebrovascular disease in a family is a contributing factor to stroke.

Enough of these signs were present so that when Andy, heeding the advice of Dr. Clawson, immediately telephoned his family physician for an appointment, the threat of stroke was closing in on him. Romson scheduled him for the following day. The doctor was disturbed to find Andy's weight back up to 217 pounds, blood pressure elevated to 176 over 100.

Romson put Andy back on his diet, prescribed a medication to control the blood pressure, and scheduled him for a complete physical the following week. By that date, the blood pressure had dropped to about normal, 144 over 80, and the visual experience had not recurred. Except for the weight, Andy seemed in good health.

Romson checked him again in two weeks. Andy had lost 10 pounds, was down to 207. By August, his next visit, he was down to 196 and his blood pressure was well under control at 136 over 80. He lost another 3 pounds by November, and it looked like he had averted the crisis. Romson scheduled him for a three-month checkup on February 17, 1977. Instead, at 6:30 p.m. on February 1, the doctor found himself outside the emergency room at Morton Plant Hospital, dispatching Amy Robertson and her two sons to the neurological intensive care unit.

To Amy's unspoken question on that ascending hospital elevator, "Why Andy?" neurologist Jackson provides an answer: "Andy Robertson had this stroke at this time because he was programmed for it. He had premature atherosclerosis, usually an inherited factor that may have been manifested by his increased triglycerides and cholesterol. He had hypertension, was overweight, smoked, and, in general, led the kind of life that contributed to his disease."

F · O · U · R

MAGNITUDE
OF THE
PROBLEM

*The number of stroke victims
a year in the United States
amounts to more than 642,000
—about 1.2 every minute.*

With the direction of a friendly nurse, Amy Robertson and her sons made their way through the sixth-floor corridors to the neurological intensive care unit. There they were given five minutes to spend with Andy. They were shocked by what they saw.

"He looked like he was barely alive," Amy says. "He had the IV in his arm and the tube in his nose and the catheter, and he was just lying there, unaware of anyone or anything."

Now Amy wanted to cry, but again she held back. It was then that she realized she had not cried since the ordeal began. "I told myself then that I'd wait until I got home, all by myself, before I cried," she says. "I didn't want to cry in front of anybody, especially my sons."

Still, even as they stood there looking at Andy's almost lifeless body, Amy told herself that he would recover. "I just had that feeling," she says. "Everything always came out right for me, so I couldn't feel any other way." They left the room and returned home to Sally and Susie, who were anxiously awaiting news about their father. Together, the family began to pass through Andy's darkest hours.

Andy's treatment in the emergency room had been typical of what a stroke patient would receive in the average community hospital. As neurologist Jackson points out, most hospitals can handle the average stroke patient. Where problems may arise, however, may be in the need for more sophisticated equipment to rule out other possible diagnoses and for the treatment of some complications, such as heart problems that might be associated with embolic stroke.

Because Andy's stroke was "completed" when he arrived at the hospital, what the doctors and nurses were treating were its effects in order to protect Andy against complications. Though some few experimental drugs and procedures aimed at minimizing damage and enhancing recovery are available on a small scale in some major medical institutions, most stroke patients continue to be treated conservatively. Immediate goals were to reduce Andy's hypertension and reduce edema, which can be expected over the first forty-eight to seventy-two hours. His airways had to be kept clear, and his respiratory system and heart had to be kept functioning normally. Complications had to be guarded against.

Although Andy did not show evidence of pain, Jackson notes that many strokes are accompanied by headache and that hemorrhagic strokes are generally associated with severe headache. Some strokes also cause abnormal or perverted sensations—such as the feeling of warmth from the touch of something cold—but, Jackson adds, **in general, stroke does not produce pain in the patient's affected limbs.**

Only about 3 percent of stroke patients have surgery, and these, according to the National Survey, are hemorrhagic patients whose physicians are trying to stem the flow of blood into or around the brain. A small number also have surgery of a carotid artery in the neck, but this operation is more often performed—and preferred—earlier in the potential stroke patient's history in an effort to prevent the stroke by reopening the narrowed artery tunnel. **The more usual treatment**, which the Robertsons observed in the ICU, **is quiet bed rest.**

Andy showed no signs of rousing on his first morning in the ICU. Dr. Romson called Amy to report the bad news: condition unchanged. She went to the hospital and sat at his bedside, holding his hand. He remained almost lifeless.

At home that night, the minister of the Baptist church she and Andy regularly attended, the Reverend Harold Morton, came to visit. He sat with the family in the living room and listened and talked. The conversation was subdued, the absence of Andy's ebullient personality evident. Amy had always been happy to sit quietly while Andy carried the conversation in a group. Now attention seemed to be focused on her, and it was not in her nature to take the dominant role—at least not yet. For the first time since Andy's attack, she began to speak of her fears and her feelings of guilt at not getting Andy to the hospital sooner. Her pastor comforted her. "He told me that Andy was just lying here in bed resting, and that that was probably all they could have done for him at the hospital," Amy says. "That made me feel better. I remember him talking to me and consoling me, and I remember the prayers." She remembers, too, going to her bedroom alone afterward and crying.

The days of the week slipped by slowly. The family returned to work or to school, Amy after three days of sitting hour after hour at Andy's bedside. But she was at the hospital daily as soon as work ended, and she remained at Andy's side each night until she was told she had to leave. "Much of the time he didn't seem conscious," she says. "He'd just lie there and squeeze my hand. He didn't know what was going on around him."

Family life, meals, housekeeping, all fell into the background. Romson called daily with progress reports, which were really reports of little or no progress. At first his message was just "guarded condition." Then the news was slightly better. "He told me they knew Andy's left side was all right, that he had suffered the damage to his right side," Amy says.

Several times at the hospital, Amy remembers the neurologist coming to talk with her. She remembers listening to him but asking no questions. Partly, the experience had been too numbing and the outcome still too uncertain. Partly, just as she had accepted the fact of Andy's stroke, so now she accepted that the doctors were in control of his life. What would she ask them? It was natural for her to depend on the strength of others—a way of life she would soon be changing dramatically.

The Robertson children also visited Andy in the ICU. "I didn't want to go, but I did want to go," Sally says, echoing much of their feelings. So she went, after she got off from work. On her first visit, when she saw Andy lying there so lifeless and unaware, she knew why she'd had reservations about going. Doug and Donald found the visits even harder.

When a loved one suffers a stroke, it is a very individual, intense, personal experience for the patient, spouse, and family. As in so many of the traumatic experiences of life, the family has a tendency to feel that they are going through it alone. They aren't. In the brief time it took you to read the preceding chapters, Americans were falling victim to stroke at the rate of more than one a minute.

Roughly 141 of every 100,000 persons across the United States will be hospitalized for an acute *initial* stroke this year or in any given year, according to the National Survey. Using April 1983 census figures, that means **almost 330,000 new stroke victims will be hospitalized in 1984.**

But that's only the beginning. That number must be increased by approximately one-third—110,000 persons—to account chiefly for victims of second or subsequent strokes. That one-third figure, says Dr. Herbert M. Baum, a National Institute demographer who was active in developing the Survey data, is based on Survey findings that 407,000 stroke patients were discharged from short-term hospitals during each of four Survey years, and approximately 299,000 of them had suffered initial strokes. The remaining 108,000 hospitalized for acute stroke had a history of previous strokes.

Combining these findings, then, the number of stroke victims hospitalized each year rises to about 440,000. Of that total, the National Institute puts the number of stroke deaths annually at about 170,000 and estimates that the nation's stroke victors form an exclusive club with a membership of almost 2,000,000.

As authoritative as the National Survey is, it is nonetheless more conservative in some of its findings than some other highly reputable sources of stroke data. The National Survey notes, for instance, that an unknown percentage of initial stroke victims were uncounted in the study because they were not hospitalized. Working with figures from a 1977 National Health Interview Survey, Dr. Baum puts the number of victims who survived their initial strokes without hospitalization at 38 percent. That adds more than 202,000 cases to the original 330,000. Combining those figures with the 110,000 hospitalized for second or subsequent strokes, the total number of stroke victims a year in the United States rises to more than 642,000— about 1.2 a minute. And undoubtedly some victims of second or subsequent strokes also were not hospitalized and are therefore uncounted.

Another source of stroke data, the government-issued *Guidelines for Stroke Care* published in 1976, puts the number of new initial stroke victims, when updated with 1980 census figures, at 500,000 a year. The National Center for Health Statistics, using its own stroke survey of 1977, concludes that the non-military non-institutionalized population of the United States with a history of stroke totals 2.7 million persons over the age of twenty, including those who suffered non-acute strokes. Data from the National Health Interview Survey and a National Survey of Nursing Homes identify a total of 2.9 million stroke victors.

These figures are not the whole story of the magnitude of stroke in the United States. The National Center for Health Statistics found that 806,000 persons were hospitalized in 1981 for "cerebrovascular disease"—stroke or conditions associated with stroke or post-stroke recovery, including TIAs, or "little strokes." Is it any wonder, then, that cerebrovascular accident, or CVA, is considered the primary neurological problem in this country and is its third leading cause of death, behind heart disease and cancer?

The following table, derived from the National Survey, gives a picture of the incidence of hospitalized new stroke victims a year by age and sex, based on April 1, 1980, U.S. Census Bureau figures for resident Americans.

ACUTE FIRST STROKES PER YEAR REQUIRING HOSPITALIZATION*

Age	Men	Women
Under 35	1,650	2,660
35 to 44	5,215	3,355
45 to 54	13,575	10,645
55 to 64	34,670	22,070
65 to 74	44,510	46,235
75 to 84	49,180	53,110
85 and over	17,025	23,415

*Rounded off to the nearest 5.

Note that the number of strokes is greater for men than for women from age thirty-five through sixty-four. Actually, on a percentage-of-population basis, strokes are primarily a male problem; the average risk of an initial stroke is 44 percent higher for men than for women. But women live longer than men, so there are more women potential stroke victims than men in the years past sixty-five. The 1980 census figures, for instance, show that there were more than 1.5 million women who were eighty-five or over compared with only about 680,000 men—yet the women had only about 6,500 more strokes.

Note also in the stroke table the "bulge" that occurs from age fifty-five to eighty-four. Because the number of cases a year rises so significantly after age fifty-five, stroke is often regarded as a problem of old age, when the vascular systems of the body have deteriorated. That's true enough, but as Andy Robertson and many other stroke victims have found out, it is the deterioration, not age itself, that increases the incidence of stroke with advancing years.

Of more immediate importance to those like the Robertsons who have already had a stroke in their family is the stroke recurrence rate. Stroke, alas, can lead to stroke, chiefly because the conditions present in the body that led to the initial stroke are still present to a greater degree than they are in the general population. That's why it's so important for post-stroke as well as potential stroke patients to keep blood pressure, weight, and other contributing factors under control.

As can be deduced from the previous data, more than 25 percent of hospitalized stroke cases a year will be patients who have a history of previous stroke. So one out of four acute stroke victims will experience stroke again in his or her lifetime. Most of those suffering recurrent strokes—80 percent, in fact—were over age sixty-five.

The statistics sound menacing, but they can be looked at from a different perspective. If only one out of four experience stroke again, according to the survey's data on hospitalized patients, then **the great majority of stroke victims, about 75 percent, never suffer another stroke; many of them recover fully or partially and go on to live satisfying and productive lives.**

The first day after a stroke is, as might be expected, the most crucial. The fact that Andy survived it was extremely encouraging. Every day of survival increased the odds of his recovery.

But Friday came and Saturday, with still no change in his condition. Already the pressures of taking charge of the family were beginning to fall on Amy. Still, every night, she was at Andy's bedside.

"From Tuesday to the following Saturday, he was really out of it," she says. She sat and held his hand every evening nonetheless. On her days off, which often fell during the week, she'd arrive at the hospital at noon and stay with him until 8:00 p.m. During these quiet hours, her mind often turned to some of the better times they'd had together.

She remembered meeting Andy at a roller rink near her home in Massachusetts. As a naval flight attendant, he flew on military air transport planes, accompanying families of servicemen and others overseas or back. He was twenty-one; she was nineteen. After they were married, they moved in with her parents to await Andy's discharge from service; because of the Korean War, he'd been frozen in for an extra year.

In August 1952, Andy was discharged, and they headed for his native Michigan, where his father had a gift waiting for them, a small home near his own. Their children grew up there over the next seventeen years. Andy became active in a civic organization, and their social lives revolved around the club's activities and their children. Amy even put in a stint as a Scout den mother. Remembering those days helped her pass the hours as Andy's condition remained unchanged.

Then, on Sunday, the change came. "Up to then, he didn't respond to anything," Dr. Romson says, "but on the sixth of February he became more alert." As his consciousness returned, Andy became aware of the tubes being used in his treatment. He signaled that he wanted the nasogastric tube removed. The ICU staff responded quickly. Andy lay in the bed as though awakening from a dream and took in the room around him. Suddenly, he was a person again, and, as the hours passed, he continued to make progress. The nurses propped him up in a sitting position in the bed. They brought baby food in and began feeding him.

It was at that moment that Amy walked in. At work all day and unaware of his improvement, she had come to the hospital ready to resume her silent bedside watch. The smile spread across her face as she walked in to see the nurse spooning pureed food into Andy's mouth. "It was the first thing he had eaten," Amy says, "and he seemed to recognize me. I knew then that he was going to make it."

F · I · V · E

A
MATTER
OF
SURVIVAL

*The best news is that the
death rate from stroke has
been declining for a decade.*

S urvival. Something inside Amy Robertson—maybe her faith in God, maybe just hope—had told her that Andy would make it through the crisis. Now the odds would begin to work for him. The survival rate for stroke is improving each year, and **studies show that stroke victims who make it through the immediate weeks after their attack live about five to seven years longer on average,** according to the National Association of Rehabilitation Facilities. Thirty percent live eleven years or more.

Of course the odds are better for ischemic stroke patients like Andy than for hemorrhagic victims, who have considerably higher mortality rates. The *Guidelines for Stroke Care* estimate that of 2,500 stroke victims per 100,000 Americans, only 625 will be hemorrhage cases—but 425 of that 625 will die within thirty days of their strokes. The IPH strokes—intraparenchymatous hemorrhages—have the highest fatality rate.

So the fact that his stroke was ischemic was in Andy's favor. The fact that he was a man, incidentally, made ischemic stroke more likely. Men have 60 percent more ischemic infarction strokes than women, and women have more than 50 percent more hemorrhagic strokes than men.

Also improving Andy's odds for long-term survival at this point was his age. Almost 65 percent of those under age sixty-five live at least a year after a stroke, as do almost 60 percent of those aged sixty-five to seventy-four and 46 percent of the seventy-five- to eighty-five-year-olds. Among those eighty-five and over, less than 30 percent survive at least another year. The same pattern can be found at the five-year survival point. Almost half of those whose strokes, like Andy's, occurred before they reached age sixty-five are still going strong five years later. The survivors drop to 35 percent of those aged sixty-five to seventy-four five years after their strokes and 22 percent of those aged seventy-five to eighty-four. Among the very old, those eighty-five years of age and older, about 7 percent survive five years or more after stroke.

So just as stroke can come suddenly at any age but is more likely among the elderly, survival favors the young but is not ruled out by advancing years.

Perhaps the best news is that **the death rate from stroke has been declining for a decade—from 214,000 in 1970 to the 1980 total of 170,000, according to the National Institute.** The exact reasons have been hard to pinpoint, but the Institute attributes much of the decline to improvements in diagnosis and treatment, especially of small strokes, to specific treatments for particular types of strokes more rapidly diagnosed after an attack, and, most particularly, to the growing awareness of the American public of the dangers of obesity, high blood pressure, smoking, and heart disease.

Researchers are also attacking stroke on many fronts today—medical, surgical, and rehabilitative. Some scientific experiments showing promise are aimed at detecting *potential* stroke, for instance, by finding weaknesses in cerebral arteries before stroke occurs. There is more emphasis today, too, by doctors in treating not just the disabilities that result from stroke but the stroke itself. For example, university researchers have been experimenting with a blood substitute that may expand blood volume and increase blood flow to the affected area of the brain when a stroke occurs, reducing stroke damage and possibly reducing or even reversing such effects as paralysis and speech disorders.

Other researchers are experimenting with infusion of other substances that show early promise of minimizing or reversing damage and hastening recovery if administered early in the course of the stroke. Cerebral artery bypass operations have been performed successfully, and their results are currently being evaluated long-term, and early management of hemorrhagic strokes is being tried experimentally.

In time, the increased attention to stroke from many quarters should bring greater progress, especially for new stroke patients.

Andy, of course, was not yet cognizant enough to consider stroke in any greater perspective than the surroundings of his own hospital bed. But Amy, like the spouses of other stroke victims who survive the immediate crisis, was already pondering a new question: In what condition would her husband survive? Guideline figures, based on a number of different studies, give this answer: **Of 1,000 stroke victims who survive the first month, 100 will be virtually unimpaired, able to return to their previous pursuits such as earning a living or keeping house. Another 400 will have some mild disability, 400 more will require special care, and 100 will require institutional care.**

Movie actress Patricia Neal is an example of one of the more prominent victims today who has made remarkable recovery from stroke. Jacquelyn Mayer Townsend, a former Miss America who suffered a stroke at age twenty-eight, is another. Former First Lady Patricia Nixon also made a comeback from stroke.

Those who are left with mild disability or even those requiring special care may still be able to pursue many of their own interests. If they are right-handed like Andy, however, they may have to learn to write and feed themselves with their left hands. Some stroke victims may no longer be able to drive a car or perform the job they held before the stroke. A cane may become as natural a part of going out for them as a raincoat in April, and a leg brace may be necessary to facilitate walking. In short, the question Amy Robertson had to face as she looked at her own recovering husband now was how much his lifestyle, her own, and their family's would have to be altered to accommodate any permanent disabilities brought on by Andy's stroke.

Actually, Andy's ICU nurses had already been active in trying to head off permanent disabilities. Care in a neurological ICU is much the same for any stroke patient, and time is always a factor. The average length of hospital stay for a stroke patient when Andy suffered his attack was just under 18 days, and that length of stay was declining. Cost-containment pressures on hospitals and new guidelines for lengths of stay for Medicare patients can be expected to speed the earlier release of more stroke patients. In 1981, for any cerebrovascular disease, the average length of stay was 12.4 days. Now the government wants the typical Medicare stroke patient out of the acute-care hospital in just under 10 days, with further treatment to be rendered in an outpatient clinic or in longer-term institutions. So rehabilitation proceeds at an accelerated pace.

The nurses' first priority had been to keep Andy under close observation. Medication to maintain his blood pressure at a normal level and to fight the edema had been flowing into him in prescribed dosages since his admission. His heart and respiration had been monitored, along with his fluid balance. The IV had provided his sustenance. Since there is no "cure" for stroke itself, the focus of the nurses was on minimizing its effects and preventing complications from arising.

Again the odds were working for Andy. Complications occur more often in patients over seventy-five, less often in patients about Andy's age or younger. The frequency of the complications also appears to be related to the type of stroke. Respiratory complications, for instance, occur in almost a third of all stroke patients, but the percentage rises if the patient is very elderly or comatose. They are also seen more frequently in hemorrhagic patients than in those like Andy who have suffered ischemic stroke.

Such complications as respiratory infection and aspiration pneumonia increase the fatality rate. In fact, it would have been safer for Andy if Amy had transported him to the hospital in an ambulance, where he could have been lying flat (or even in Susie's flat-bottomed pickup truck if it had been available), than in a car where he was sitting up. It would also have made mouth-to-mouth resuscitation easier if it had been necessary. Ambulance attendants, in addition to monitoring a patient's vital signs, also make certain the patient's airways remain clear. Nurses in the ICU place equal importance on that need because asphyxia is a common risk of stroke to be guarded against, particularly in patients who are stuporous or unconscious.

The ICU nurses had been exercising Andy's arms and legs for him— since he was still incapable of exercising himself—in order to prevent contractures, which are the permanent shortening of stroke-affected muscles, and to prevent immobilized joints. Even while Andy was lying unconscious in bed, nurses regularly moved each of his arms and legs through a series of range-of-motion exercises. While contractures occur in only about 3 percent of cases, decubitis ulcers—better known as bedsores—occur in about 15 percent. So ICU nurses had also been moving Andy's body in bed frequently to prevent them.

Once Andy's consciousness was restored, one of the primary things the nurses were concerned with was his feeding. Ordinarily, because of the paralysis to one side of their throats, stroke patients have difficulty swallowing. The problem usually occurs regardless of which side of the brain is affected. Physicians note that the first stage of swallowing is voluntary and that once the food is back in the throat, the swallowing becomes automatic. Only the voluntary aspect is affected by the stroke. The patients handle liquids poorly because of their lack of physical control. Like Andy, they generally have to be started on baby foods and on jello, custards, oatmeal, and other foods they find it easier to master. Some patients have to be tube-fed—baby-type foods placed in a bag and allowed to drip slowly through a tube into the patient's stomach. Some never get used to eating; most, however, learn quickly to direct the food to the side of their throat that is not paralyzed and look to gravity for assistance in swallowing it.

In Andy's case, swallowing was no problem—though feeding himself was. From that first day of alertness, he was able to eat whatever was fed to him. The problem was that Andy suffered from spatial disorientation; he couldn't put a finger into his mouth, much less a spoonful of food. The problem is far from uncommon, and families of some stroke patients find it difficult to watch their recovering patients try to feed themselves because the patients become so messy. But, some ICU nurses at Morton Plant Hospital explain, anything the patient can do for himself will help him restore his self-confidence and his sense of worth. So it is better that he look messy and gain self-esteem than that he be neat because someone else takes over the feeding role. For Andy, however, the disorientation was so great that coping with it became a job for his therapists—a job with which Amy soon found herself involved.

Andy's stay in the ICU after regaining consciousness was brief, as is usually the case with stroke patients who are recovering well from ischemic attacks; some cases, however, especially hemorrhagic patients, who often need lengthy close observation, have prolonged stays. So once again it was one of those small events that signaled great progress to Amy when, only a few days after she had first found him propped up in bed, Amy arrived at the hospital to find that Andy had been moved to a room on the neurological care floor. The move seemed to assure her with visible evidence that survival had been accomplished. Recovery was the new goal.

S · I · X

THE
EFFECTS
OF
STROKE

*Degrees of recovery vary
from almost no recovery
to almost complete recovery.*

STROKE REHABILITATION SPECIALIST

A ndy's stroke had severely damaged the left side of his brain, making him a "right hemiplegic," one of two main categories by which stroke patients are differentiated. He had suffered paralysis of the right half of his body—his right arm, his right leg, the right half of his throat and tongue. In less severe cases, or after there has been some recovery, the disability may also be referred to as "right hemiparesis"—a milder or incomplete paralysis.

Left hemiplegia or left hemiparesis, of course, would mean that the left half of a patient's body was affected as a result of stroke damage to the right side of the brain.

Because cells had been killed in the motor speech center of his brain, Andy's ability to speak was affected, as is common in right hemiplegics. The degree of the infarction—that is, the extent of cell death—determines the degree of speech disability. Because Andy could say a word or two right from the start of his recovery, chiefly the word "you," which he used in response to almost everything that was said to him, he was initially diagnosed as "dysphasic." But the terms "dysphasia" and "aphasia" have been used pretty interchangeably in his case, as they often are in stroke cases.

Aphasia refers to the patient's inability to talk or to understand language spoken to him, or both. It's called expressive aphasia when the difficulty is in the patient's ability to speak, receptive aphasia if the difficulty is in his ability to understand. That understanding usually applies to both the spoken and the written word. Receptive aphasia is the more difficult for the family and other caregivers to deal with because the patient has a problem understanding even the most simple of instructions.

Dysphasia, the less severe form of this language difficulty, may be accompanied by slow and inadequate tongue movements, accumulations of secretions in the mouth, frequent choking, emotional changes, and poor articulation of words.

Sensory deprivation is another result of stroke that can arise out of a patient's inability to speak or understand language. Consider for a moment how Andy felt when he awoke in a hospital bed that Sunday and found he was unable to communicate with anyone or to understand what anyone was saying. That's the condition in which stroke patients, particularly in the days and weeks immediately after their attacks, often live. Any wonder, then, that Andy showed confusion in his new surroundings? Some patients also suffer from irritability, restlessness, and hallucinations and/or delusions, especially if they continue to be confined to bed. Night can accentuate their feelings of deprivation and lead to further restlessness. So can overstimulation, such as a roomful of visitors who all seem to be staring and speaking in a foreign language.

One of those who felt the communication problem with Andy immediately was his cousin Jim Murphy, who flew down from Michigan when he learned of the stroke about a week or so after he'd left Andy at the airport. Murphy took his turn with Amy and other family members and friends at Andy's bedside after Andy had regained consciousness. "I never knew for sure that he was understanding me," Murphy says. "I'd talk with him, and he'd laugh and smile, but no words were spoken by him. I really didn't know if he knew what I was talking about. I'd think: 'I wonder if he really knows I'm here. I wonder if he knows who I am.' I'd shake his hand and say: 'Hey, do you remember this, do you remember that?' He'd smile and shake his head yes. It was almost like he pretended, like he would have reacted the same way to anything I said."

Andy's real estate associate, Marv Chester, visited almost every night once Andy was moved out of the ICU and sometimes brought his children with him. His memories of trying to communicate with Andy in those early post-stroke days are much like Jim Murphy's: He saw Andy there in body but not in mind.

Frightening, isn't it? It was to the loved ones of Andy Robertson. Andy's neurologist, Dr. Jackson, notes that the effects of stroke can be devastating and catastrophic. Andy had right-side paralysis, couldn't express himself, appeared unable to truly understand others. It was natural that he could become upset, frustrated, and agitated. Some patients require anti-anxiety agents to cope with these problems.

Both the brain damage caused by the stroke and the frustrations resulting from the effects of stroke can alter a patient's personality. Loss of emotional control is one of the chief changes, particularly in the early stages of recovery. Andy cried frequently for no apparent reason, and, as his recovery progressed, he became subject to outbursts of temper, which Amy attributes mostly to impatience, something he did not show before his stroke.

It was impossible for those around him to know at that time the thoughts that might be going through his mind. Jackson and others in the field feel that the depression he exhibited at times is an effect more often brought on by frustration than by actual damage to the brain. Was he aware and concerned about a loss of body image as a result of his paralysis? The younger the stroke patient, the greater this sense of loss. "Stroke patients worry about whether they will ever have sex again with a spouse, whether they will ever be continent, self-supporting," an ICU nurse at Morton Plant Hospital explains. "It's a heavy load for them to carry." It can be especially heavy if their disabilities render them unable to articulate their fears.

Progress in recovery and the supportive attitude of a family can improve the situation, as, indeed, Andy's case proves. Amy and the family soon learned to expect Andy's outbursts of crying that bore no relation to the situation and to change the subject of the moment as a means of distracting him and dealing with his outbursts. But Amy never got used to them. Even knowing that his outbursts resulted directly from his lack of emotional control as a result of the stroke, Amy found the experience of seeing Andy in tears always difficult to accept.

Usually at the early stages of recovery, changes in mental functions and personality characteristics occur regardless of the type of stroke suffered. But as time passes, changes may vary in type and degree or gradually disappear, according to which side of the brain is damaged.

The American Heart Association points out that right hemiplegics like Andy tend to have memory difficulties associated with language. Left hemiplegics have more general memory difficulties, particularly those associated with space and time perception—though again these may be seen in any stroke patient at an early stage of recovery.

Andy's frequent use of the word "you" in response to any attempt at communication is an example of the difficulty right hemiplegics have in remembering language. Other stroke patients respond with what speech therapists describe as a "word salad." Ask them a question, and they may reply with a mixture of words that have no relation to the question or, for that matter, that make no sense at all. Yet the stroke victim may feel that he is answering the question properly. His brain fails to tell him that the words he's using are not appropriate. He may also be frustrated by the failure of those around him to understand his answer and therefore may find them repeating a question that, in his mind, he has already answered.

Because Andy was right-handed, chances were almost 100 percent that his dominant hemisphere would be the left side of his brain. The undamaged right hemisphere, which is related to spontaneous, automatic types of responses, then took a greater role in responding in matters of language. The result was that in addition to "you" and, not long afterward, "yes" and "no" (which also might have no relation to the question asked or be the reverse of the appropriate answer), he also sometimes used automatic or spontaneous language—language over which a stroke patient has little or no control.

Sometimes the words he blurted out were the four-letter kind that embarrassed Amy and their family. Why such words come to be used commonly by such stroke patients is unknown, except that they are part of the automatic response mechanism. The patient may not even be aware he is saying them.

One speech-language therapist tells the story of three stroke patients whom she took out for dinner at a Chinese restaurant. One patient, a man, could say only three words—"show," "shit," and "I." When the proprietor came to their table after the meal and asked how they had liked their dinner, this patient wanted to express his appreciation. He looked at the proprietor, smiled broadly, and said "Shit."

Not only was the proprietor offended, but so was one of the other patients, a woman. The language therapist found herself trying to soothe injured feelings and explain the problem.

The patient who had made the unfortunate choice of words was about the same age as Andy Robertson, and the therapist had been working with him to control his language. "It's usually stroke patients who are very limited in their verbalizations who say such things," she says. "This patient wanted to be able to say something to express his appreciation, and any word that came out was satisfying to him. As he improved in therapy and as his vocabulary increased to about twenty or twenty-five words, he was able to control his language." Meanwhile, as Amy learned in trying to help Andy, the lesson is that you can expect a stroke patient to say almost anything, and you can't blame him if what he says isn't what you'd like to hear.

There are other changes that began to be evidenced in Andy as a result of his right hemiplegia. Andy had always been energetic and active. But right hemiplegics, whatever their previous nature, tend to become slow and cautious in undertaking anything and in responding to questions and commands. Had he been a left hemiplegic, his response would have been just the opposite. Left hemiplegics become rash and impulsive. Because their speech may not be impaired, they may also give the impression of greater capability than they actually have, which could give rise to situations dangerous to themselves and others.

In that sense, the odds were still working for Andy, since many therapists feel that the left hemiplegic is more difficult to rehabilitate—and to live with—than the right. Left hemiplegics who have suffered a massive stroke have difficulty determining where they are in terms of time and space. They are confused; they have greater difficulty in learning to dress because sometimes they feel no relation to their body parts. They do not remember instructions or even very recent experiences.

As one rehabilitation nurse explains, many of these patients know that something is wrong with them and with their thought processes, but they don't know how to deal with that. "You can carry on a perfectly rational conversation with a left hemiplegic," she says, "and he'll promise you, for example, that he won't get out of bed. Two minutes later, he's flat on his face on the floor. His judgment is gone, he's very impulsive, and he doesn't remember the conversation. It's hard for families or spouses who are not aware of this problem to understand that the patient is not just being purposely nasty. It frustrates families just as it frustrates the professionals."

What makes it difficult to understand, she adds, is the fact that the left hemiplegic may be very sociable and more aesthetically acceptable than a right hemiplegic like Andy, with his obvious disabilities. That can be disarming to his caregivers. Andy's slower, more cautious attitude minimized the dangers of his new situation to himself. But a left hemiplegic may appear to have reasonable judgment and then, moments later, propel himself along a hospital corridor in a wheelchair with no regard to the fact that people might be in his way. Families must be aware, she points out, that the left hemiplegic is a real safety problem.

One left hemiplegic, somewhat younger than Andy Robertson, appeared to have made a full recovery from his stroke after a relatively short period. He had no residual paralysis and could communicate fluently. But he had no memory of events from day to day. If a nurse asked him why he was in the hospital, he might reply that he was there for back surgery or that he had undergone back surgery. A stroke? He had no memory of it. Nor would he remember the following day conversing with that nurse. This "retention span" problem is not uncommon with any stroke patient, but it is particularly common with left hemiplegics. Andy, while he does not remember the actual experience of having a stroke or the immediate days and even weeks afterward, grew to understand what had happened to him and what his disabilities were as a result. A left hemiplegic, on the other hand, could easily forget he'd suffered paralysis of one leg, say, and he might assure you he was capable of driving a car. Rashly, he would get to his feet to walk to the car and demonstrate his ability to drive, only to fall after he'd taken a step. Why did he fall? He might say his leg was asleep. The same scene might be repeated on any subsequent day.

Because of their forgetfulness and their difficulty in relating to the parts of their own bodies, left hemiplegics also have trouble in personal grooming and in performing the activities of daily living. An added problem may be altered visual perception, which may occur regardless of which side of the body is affected.

Andy, for instance, a right hemiplegic, had a reduced field of vision to his right side. If he was wheeled from one hospital department to another, unless he turned his head fully he'd be likely to see only one side of the corridor. On his return he might become confused because he felt he was traveling a different route; he was seeing the corridor's other side. But as his recovery progressed, he could be made to understand what was causing that confusion.

A left hemiplegic with a visual defect would be more inclined to shave one side of his face and ignore the other—and believe that he had groomed himself properly. In fact, he might forget whether he had shaved at all and assure anyone who questioned him that he had—or hadn't. The forgetfulness itself, on the simplest level, might lead him to leave the water running in the bathroom or to use the toilet but not flush it.

Andy Robertson and his fellow right hemiplegics, then, had to be coaxed and encouraged to overcome their cautionary attitude, while their counterparts, the left hemiplegics, had to be watched carefully and guided in their every activity. Efforts also had to be made to stem their impulsiveness. Therapists say that extracting a promise of more rational behavior from a left hemiplegic is often a worthless endeavor because the moment you leave the patient, he may not remember the promise. He is constantly endangered by his rashness, his lack of memory, and his inability to judge speed, distance, time, and space. Andy had a far better chance of recovery from some of those problems than could be expected of a left hemiplegic.

We will consider many of the effects of stroke in more depth as we deal with the various types of stroke therapy in detail in later chapters. Meanwhile, how do Amy Robertson and the spouses of other stroke victims begin to cope with the problems of aphasia and dysphasia in their mates?

Amy received printed literature at Morton Plant Hospital, which she shared with her children, on the effects of aphasia and how to help Andy overcome them. The American Heart Association has published a number of instructive booklets on stroke, and, in all cases, families of stroke victims need information and education if they are to be able to provide their loved ones with the special compensations and constant encouragement needed. The Heart Association literature dealing with recovery from aphasia stresses that, in the long run, "the family is the foundation upon which recovery depends. The best way the family can help is to offer stimulating and understanding companionship."

Of course you will need good professional assistance, but there is much you yourself can do for the patient. Here, quoted with permission, are some of the guidelines the AHA offers:

Discover how well the patient communicates through professional testing and your own observations. **Engage the patient in conversation, ask him many questions, and don't accept a nod of his head as sufficient proof of understanding.**

Spend time with the patient when he is most responsive. In the early stages, keep these efforts brief. As he recovers, they can be lengthened.

Leave him alone for portions of the day, perhaps watching television, so he can develop self-assurance.

Don't let him stagnate, but start with one or two selected visitors.

Make a checklist of his special interests, and use it when you or others are going to spend time with him.

Watch closely for unfavorable responses, and don't be discouraged by setbacks.

Change the subject or leave him alone if he gets upset or fidgety.

Accept him as he is at the moment, reminding yourself that he has less control over his feelings than you do and real cause for frustration.

Include him in family affairs, treating him as much as possible as you did before he became ill.

Keep him in touch with what the family does, and let him know he's still an important member.

Try moving him up to a slightly higher level of speech and understanding by talking at that level and helping him do the same.

If he can't name objects, use phrases, or make sentences:

Put an object in front of him and write or say its name while touching the object.

Approve his efforts to communicate by some sign.

If his pronunciation is poor at first, accept it. You can correct his mistakes later as he improves.

Avoid set drills and exercises, such as saying the alphabet; vary what you do with him.

Help him improve his vocabulary—nouns first, verbs next—and omit words he has trouble with.

Encourage him to talk, talk, talk!

If he can't follow conversations or instructions:

Use short simple sentences, even words or phrases, in discussing a topic of interest to him, and point to an object you're discussing.

Stop the conversation if he gets stuck and go back to the first part of your remark.

Use concrete words—bread instead of food, leg instead of limb.

If he has trouble reading or writing:

Have him copy headlines out of a newspaper or magazine.

Let him print the words in large letters.

Help him to read aloud the words he has copied.

Get him a simple book, preferably with large type, and read it aloud with him.

Let him try to read by himself as soon as possible.

Remember, the Heart Association says, a substitute companion can give you the chance for rest and recreation and be a beneficial change for him, too. Talking with others who have similar problems may also be helpful to you.

In a patient with right hemiplegia, the Heart Association offers this advice:

Don't underestimate the patient's ability to learn and communicate even if he can't use speech. Try other forms of communication, such as pantomime and demonstration. Don't overestimate his understanding of speech. Don't shout; keep your messages simple and brief; don't use special voices. Divide tasks into simple steps and give many indications of progress.

For a left hemiplegic, the advice is as follows:

Don't overestimate his abilities. Use verbal clues if he has difficulty with demonstration. Break tasks into small steps and give much feedback. Watch to see what he can do safely rather than taking his word for it. Minimize clutter around him and avoid rapid movement around him.

For a patient with one-sided neglect, more common in left hemiplegics:

Keep the unimpaired side toward the action. Avoid trapping the patient in an unnecessarily confined area. Avoid nagging, but give frequent clues to aid orientation. Provide reminders of the neglected side. Arrange his environment to maximize his performance.

For a patient with memory problems:

Establish a fixed routine whenever possible. Keep messages short to fit his retention span. Present new information one step at a time. Allow the patient to finish one step before proceeding to the next. Give frequent indications of progress; he might forget his successes. Train in settings that resemble the setting where his behavior will be used. Use memory aids such as appointment books, written notes, and schedule cards. Use familiar objects and old associations when teaching new tasks.

Because stroke affects only a part of the brain and affects it in varying degrees in different patients, behavior and recovery may be different in each patient. In estimating recovery, neurologist Jackson cites the "Rule of Three": In three days you'll have an idea of how well the patient will recover; in three weeks, you'll have a good idea; and in three months, you'll know. Like others in the field, he notes that most spontaneous recovery takes place within the first three months and certainly within the first six months. But some progress often continues to be made beyond that point and even years later.

As a physician who specializes in stroke rehabilitation at a major medical center put it: "Degrees of recovery vary from almost no recovery to almost complete recovery. Some persons can recover from what looks like a very severe stroke and, through retraining, go back to driving a car and to their former occupations. Usually, however, with a severe stroke, they do not recover to that extent."

S · E · V · E · N

THE
STROKE
TEAM

*High-quality rehabilitation is best
delivered by a closely integrated
team composed of the family
physician, medical specialists,
nurses, therapists, social worker,
dietitian, rehabilitation counselor,
speech pathologist, psychologist,
the patient's family,
and the patient.*

GUIDELINES FOR STROKE CARE

Once Andy was capable of being fed that first meal of baby food, he became a candidate for rehabilitation. At Morton Plant Hospital, as at a still-growing number of hospitals today, that rehabilitation was the job of "the stroke team."

The stroke team is composed of health-care professionals in various therapies and fields whose purpose is not only to rehabilitate a patient like Andy but to help his wife and family deal with the social and financial problems associated with stroke.

To take advantage of the team's services, Andy had to be referred by his physician, who also is a team member. Some physicians still prefer to direct the rehabilitation themselves, calling in a speech therapist or a physical therapist, for instance, as they perceive the need. Also, some acute-care hospitals, particularly smaller ones, may not have the full services that a team employs. The recovering patient may have to be referred to a longer-term rehabilitation facility in the community. But the stroke team concept has taken hold and can be expected to increase in importance as these therapists continue to show the beneficial results of their services. One has only to observe team members working with stroke-disabled patients like Andy to appreciate their value.

The basic principle of stroke rehabilitation is to begin therapy as soon as possible. The progress of the patient can be remarkably swift, especially considering the devastated condition in which patients are often brought to the emergency room. Let's take a look at the members of the team and at the various individual therapies and therapists who take part in the rehabilitation process.

FAMILY PHYSICIAN

As primary-care physician, Dr. Romson put Andy's rehabilitation process in motion. In the early days of family doctor–team collaboration, the therapists were obliged to submit each recommendation for care to the primary doctor for his approval. Because that usually resulted in a delay of a day or two in the rehabilitation process, pioneers in team care worked with the medical staffs of hospitals to obtain a more autonomous position. In Andy's case, as in many instances today, team members are able to proceed with their various therapies without family doctor approval of each new step. Of course, Romson would see the progress notes entered into Andy's medical record from day to day and receive a weekly report on the team's goals and accomplishments. He could modify Andy's treatment according to his own evaluation.

Both Andy and Amy feel they were fortunate to have a physician who was keen on rehabilitation therapy. Some doctors are less enthusiastic, feeling that stroke patients will recover naturally at their own speed and to their own maximum degree of progress. They regard a formal rehabilitation program as an unnecessary expense for the patient and the insurer. As a director of rehabilitation services at a major hospital explains: "Some physicians feel that their stroke patients will get better eventually no matter what. They'll let a patient lie in bed; then, when it seems appropriate to them, they'll get him up into a chair. Again after some undetermined length of time, they'll try him to see if he can stand. If he can, they'll try walking him, all without any specific therapy. Physicians also have their individual preferences. Some never refer a patient to stroke rehab at all. One doctor may feel that physical therapy is important but occupational therapy isn't. Or a doctor might feel that speech therapy is of no value for at least the first month or two after stroke."

A growing number of doctors, however, automatically refer their stroke patients to the team as soon as the patient is admitted, in the firm belief that rehabilitation can improve recovery and reduce mortality and that the sooner it is implemented the better.

NEUROLOGIST
Because of his specialist expertise in cerebrovascular disease, **the neurologist usually serves as medical advisor to the stroke team.** Dr. Jackson determined Andy's neurological status, physical condition, capabilities, and, with Dr. Romson, the diagnosis. He provided the neurological work-up—which today may involve the newer scanning techniques—and he participated in team meetings concerned with Andy's needs and progress.

PHYSIATRIST
Though they are limited in number, these physicians specialize in physical medicine and rehabilitation. They are more likely to be available at large medical centers, where they evaluate the stroke patient's functional abilities, both present and potential, prescribe specialized forms of treatment based on each patient's special needs and resources, and coordinate the activities of team members.

NURSES
Andy's rehabilitation therapy actually was begun by the ICU nurses even before he had regained consciousness when they started moving his limbs through range-of-motion exercises. Their first concern during the acute stage of his illness was simply keeping him alive, but stroke patients must be managed with the anticipation that their neurological damage will persist and that, therefore, measures must be taken from the start to prevent secondary, avoidable difficulties. With no time to spare, then, the nurses went to work on specific routine activities from the time of Andy's admission.

During those first critical days in the ICU, they monitored his pulmonary, cardiac, and excretory functions and exercised his muscles and joints. They were responsible for correctly positioning him in the bed to safeguard his disabled limbs and for turning him every two hours as well as stimulating him when he became conscious and started to show growing awareness. The shifting of his body in the bed was extremely important to prevent bedsores. These are even more of a threat in frail elderly patients because of pressure on their thin, bony frames. The nurses' movement of Andy's body in the bed also was aimed at improving his circulation and respiration.

Nurses, as in Andy's case, also are usually the first to put the patient through the passive range-of-motion exercises, exercising his arms and legs for him before he is able to exercise them himself. They raised and lowered Andy's limbs and put them through a series of motions aimed at keeping his muscles and joints loose. As he began to show improvement, they assisted him in active range-of-motion exercises, in which he performed the same exercises himself with their guidance and assistance as needed.

The roles of nurses range through the activities of many of the therapies, especially in the early stages of a patient's recovery. They keep him from suffering deformities from atrophying muscles and, as he progresses, they assist him in performing his activities of daily living, instruct him in transfers such as from bed to wheelchair, and help him in walking again. They not only save lives, but, by their functions, shorten recovery time.

In small hospitals, especially where a social service department is not fully developed, the nurse may contribute to the continuity of care by making appropriate referrals to community services.

REHABILITATION NURSE
Ideally, the stroke team includes a nurse specially skilled in the rehabilitation process. She **makes early contact with the patient to assure prompt referral to the hospital-based services he needs, and she works with the general nursing staff and the rehabilitation team to make sure the patient's program is being followed.** She initiates staff conferences with his physicians and rehabilitation specialists, trains nurse's aides, practical nurses, and others— including spouses like Amy and their families—in care designed to restore the patient's mobility. She also helps the family in its involvement with discharge planning and social service. Very often, due in part to the small numbers of physiatrists, she will serve as coordinator of the stroke team, responsible for making all the therapies come together for the greatest benefit of the patient.

PHYSICAL THERAPIST
Andy's functional motor abilities, his joint mobility, and the reasons for his limitations of motion all became the concern of his physical therapist. Usually **one of the first therapists to reach a patient's bedside, the physical**

therapist does a thorough evaluation, noting any sensory problems that might hinder successful rehabilitation efforts.

At Morton Plant Hospital today, when the physical therapist has completed his assessment, he makes a multiple-copy report of his findings and sends a copy to each team member. The whole team is thereby made aware that the patient has been referred to the stroke service, and the various other therapists begin scheduling their own evaluations in light of the physical therapist's findings.

Andy's exercise program, aimed at enhancing return of muscle function, was a challenge for a physical therapist. The exercises are a form of "patterning" designed to get the patient's nervous system active again. The therapist evaluated Andy's active motion and stimulated specific muscle groups that were functioning, such as by having him move his head, roll over, sit up, achieve sitting balance, and eventually be able to transfer from his bed to a chair, to a wheelchair, and so on.

The physical therapist picked up on the passive range-of-motion exercises started by the nurses and proceeded to the active ones as well, also instructing Andy in the rationale and methods of the treatment program. Andy continued to improve his alertness and performance slowly with the aid of the therapists and the encouragement of Amy and his family and friends. "At this stage," Dr. Romson says, "he became more interested in wanting to improve himself, and he was really willing to work at it quite hard." So he responded well to the strengthening exercises aimed at getting him mobile again, first in a wheelchair and later on his feet. Overall, the therapist worked with the nursing staff in providing the rehabilitation practices of good patient management and worked with other team members in formulating and carrying out an effective and comprehensive plan of care.

OCCUPATIONAL THERAPIST

Just as the physical therapist worked with Andy's muscles to restore their function, so the **occupational therapist's role was to work with his performance of daily tasks, especially taking into consideration Andy's overlapping problems such as altered vision, speech-understanding, and impairments in sensation.** This therapist's evaluation focused on Andy's loss of feeling on his damaged side, his general awareness, and his ability once again to resume his activities of daily living, activities he took so much for granted before his stroke.

Often stroke victims with the perseverance to become stroke victors learn to perform functions with the left hand that many persons could do only with the use of two hands. Andy's own feats at a later stage of his recovery were sometimes extraordinary, but stories of such feats abound. One New York woman, for instance, who suffered her first stroke just before her eighteenth birthday, married within three years of her stroke, gave birth to two daughters over the next several years, and learned to diaper, feed, and care for them using only her left hand. She cooked for her family, cared for her husband, and maintained her home. At age forty, and after a second stroke, she has also served as president of a local stroke club and continues to be active in it.

The patient's ability to perform such various tasks and his or her ability to follow instructions and to remember them also come under the guidance of the occupational therapist. The occupational therapist develops a positive program of functional activities and self-care for the patient, also teaching the use of self-care assistive devices. For example, Andy was taught to use a special table knife that enabled him to cut meat on his plate himself using only one hand. The therapists also advise patients in other aspects of using their unimpaired arm, such as in dressing, buttoning a jacket with the left hand, and so on. In addition, they advise families about modifications that might be needed in their homes to accommodate the patient's disabilities and instruct spouses and families so that they will be able to assist the patient in further learning at home.

SOCIAL WORKER

Amy's financial problems, especially now with Andy hospitalized, brought her into contact with the social worker, **a team member whose goal is to assess the social and financial needs of the patient and family as well as their psychological needs.** She knows the community services available, learns the economic resources of the patient, and tries to fit the two together. On one of Amy's visits to the hospital, the social worker met with her to discuss possible sources of supplementary income as well as planning for Andy's continued care after his discharge from the hospital. She referred Amy to the Social Security Administration office in the community. The social worker is prepared to help patients in finding assistance through their community resources. He or she attends staff conferences, maintains close communication with the team, and apprises the physicians and other team members of all social problems that might hinder or prolong recovery.

SPEECH THERAPIST

We have already seen a good deal of the language-communication problems that may be experienced by stroke patients with Andy's disabilities. Resolution or at least some improvement in these problems is the goal of the speech therapist—one of whom started working with Andy right at bedside, which, in turn, prompted Amy to begin to repeat the therapy with Andy, based on her observations of the therapist's work. **The speech therapist, or speech pathologist, as he or she is also called, evaluates communication difficulties, initiates speech therapy when appropriate, provides consultation to the patient, the staff, and the family, uses various methods of** language stimulation we will consider later, and suggests methods of language stimulation and communication to the family.

VOCATIONAL REHABILITATION COUNSELOR
In a small hospital, the functions of this team member may be assumed by the social worker. The extent of Andy's disabilities ruled out any immediate return to employment, but it is the counselor's role to interview the family and, if possible, the patient in order to uncover social, psychological, and vocational problems. She provides counseling, if appropriate, to patient and family during hospitalization, and she keeps the team informed regarding family relations and any situations that might reduce maximum vocational rehabilitation.

CORRECTIVE THERAPIST
Andy's contacts with a corrective therapist were still further ahead in his rehabilitation process. This type of therapist is more often found at federal rehabilitative facilities, such as VA hospitals, than at community hospitals. He generally has a background in physical education and is physically capable of dealing with men of large size. The corrective therapist is responsible for various rehabilitation exercises, muscle strengthening, training in walking, and orthopedics. He helps the patient to learn conditioning exercises and exercises using the large muscles of the arms and legs.

While these are the regular participants of the stroke team, others in the hospital may serve as consultants and as they are needed for the care of individual patients. In some cases, for instance, a dietitian may be called in to help a patient with a nutritional problem or a psychiatrist or clergyman may be consulted for a patient with social or psychological problems. Recreational therapists also are available at some major medical institutions.

Andy's stroke team met weekly to discuss its patients, their needs, and their progress and to integrate the workings of each form of therapy. Andy's condition, for instance, precluded physical therapy when he was first admitted, so his nurses managed his initial care and the social services worker initiated contact with Amy regarding their non-medical problems. With time in the hospital at a premium—and likely to grow shorter under the increasing pressure for cost-containment today—the stroke team tries to make maximum use of it for the patient's advantage. At the weekly meetings, each member of the team reports, and the team comes to a consensus regarding each patient's long-term and short-term goals. A copy of Andy's report went regularly to Romson. For the most part, doctors find themselves in agreement with what the team recommends.

Often the stroke team is an asset to the family physician as well as to the patient and the family in terms of its knowledge of community resources.

More than physicians, who often are not familiar with all the services in their communities, social services workers can be of great assistance in this area.

Ben Kraus, rehabilitation services manager at Morton Plant Hospital, cites three major factors as influencing a stroke patient's recovery:

1. The individual patient himself—how he reacts to the disability.

2. The patient's family and the type of support it offers the stroke patient.

3. The availability of the various rehabilitation therapies.

Andy had all three assets working for him. As the Reverend Morton, a frequent visitor, recalls the therapy: "I watched them tirelessly and patiently show him words. I didn't know if he would ever make progress because it seemed so slow at first. But he had a good spirit and he worked with them, and his attitude was good even during that period." Moreover, Reverend Morton adds, "the family didn't fall to pieces. They were emotionally touched, but they took it well."

Amy also was making some observations about Andy during this period that she later was to apply to stroke patients in general: "At first they don't have the motivation to do things. Then, as they recover, they keep thinking of new things they want to do."

Providing that motivation is part of the role of the stroke team. As Kraus notes, initially patients show a lot of natural improvement—improvement they would show even if they had no assistance. But in the long run, he says, the patient is not going to get nearly as well as he would with therapy because therapy offers a sense of direction, established rehabilitation techniques, and repetition to make those techniques effective.

Typically, a patient like Andy in the early stages of recovery might be started on rehabilitation every other day if his endurance is poor. As his endurance improves and, perhaps, as his family physician feels he is ready for the stimulation to be reinforced, the therapy may begin on a daily basis. Some therapies, physical therapy especially, may be given twice a day. In coordinating the activities, the stroke team may start the patient with speech therapy in the morning, when he is freshest, and then let him progress to the other therapies later in the day.

Spouse support groups are another form of family therapy that has received more and more attention in recent years. These groups serve a number of functions: They give spouses the opportunity to ask questions that have been bothering them or to hear their questions asked by others if they themselves are too shy to ask. **They offer spouses counseling and consolation at a time when it is most needed, and, by their nature, they show spouses that they are not alone with their problems.** Where they sometimes fall short—as they did in Amy Robertson's case—is that they often hold their meetings at the hospital during the day, when working spouses of stroke victims find it difficult to attend. Amy went to only one such meeting, though she would have willingly gone to many if her work schedule had allowed.

Spouses like Amy, as anyone working in the stroke field realizes, need emotional support and instruction as much as their stroke-disabled loved ones do. As Amy learned, the information provided in the hours and days immediately following the stroke are often lost in the confusion and upheaval surrounding the trauma. The same information, provided at a later, calmer time, can bring comfort and valuable assistance.

Stroke specialists are quick to point out that the more the spouse knows about the situation she or he has to deal with, the better she will be able to deal with it, so spouses should take every opportunity to inquire and learn. When Amy found that spouse support group meetings did not fit into her work schedule, she obtained booklets from the hospital that helped her understand, and cope with, Andy's aphasia and other effects of his stroke. No spouse needs to remain in the dark with so many sources of light available.

If there is one question that runs through a spouse's mind after a stroke in the family, it is probably the same question most often raised at spouse support group meetings: "How long is my husband (or wife) going to remain this way?" On the very first night of Andy's stroke, you will recall, Amy arbitrarily fixed the length of that period at one year—"in a year he'll be fine." Actually, there is no fixed period one can point to for recovery. As we've already noted, a stroke patient's most significant progress will probably be made in the first three months and up to the first six months after stroke. Also, the "Rule of Three" indicates that after three months you should more or less know the potential extent of his recovery. But you must also keep in mind the importance of the patient's motivation and the family's support—factors that Andy had in good supply. Recovery must be dealt with on an individual basis.

Because the length of hospital stay keeps dropping, the stroke patient is usually discharged from the hospital in about two weeks or less. By that time the stroke team should know enough about you and your home environment and the needs of the patient to recommend the next step—whether you should take the patient directly home and utilize some home-care services or the outpatient department of the hospital or whether he should spend some time in a rehabilitation unit or facility or a skilled nursing institution.

Whatever course is recommended, further therapy is generally necessary. In fact, the *Guidelines* **stipulate that the rehabilitation process must not stop at the time of discharge,** that discharge planning and post-hospital care are crucial, and that physicians and other health professionals should actively involve the family through "full, frank, and realistic explanation and discussion of the patient's condition at all times, the purpose of specific procedures undertaken, ultimate prognosis for recovery, probable permanent limitations and deficits as these become established," and the steps necessary to adapt to residual damage. "The family," say the *Guidelines*, "is the most important resource available to the stroke patient and his physician in every phase of rehabilitation."

Amy Robertson would add one more resource to call on: God. "Without God," she says, "I would never have been able to keep going."

More and more, reserved Amy was becoming Andy's voice. It was not an arrangement she accepted easily, but, with growing strength, it was one to which she was resolved to accustom herself.

E · I · G · H · T

THE
BEGINNINGS
OF
RECOVERY

*We're trying to stimulate
as many areas of the brain
as possible.*

SPEECH THERAPIST ANN MOSS
Morton F. Plant Hospital
Clearwater, Florida

B y now the news of Andy's stroke had spread to all his associates, and visitors to his hospital room were frequent. In fact, so many of Andy's children, friends, and relatives came to see him that Amy grew concerned. "Only two persons were supposed to be visiting any patient in a room at one time," she says, "because it was a four-bed room. But when we all used to get together there, all the children and I coming at once, we used to get so noisy. The hospital had unlimited visiting hours, so we used to stay a long time. Other patients complained about us, but it seemed to help Andy for us to be there, so we visited and stayed."

Neighbors also tried to help out. They sent "get well" cards; they sent fried chicken dinners over to Amy; they offered financial help, which, she says, she was too proud to accept, though she wished dearly they would have forced it on her. They also got involved in her efforts to transfer Andy to the Veterans Administration Medical Center at Bay Pines, Florida. Her reason was that in addition to the physical and emotional problems of stroke, Amy was now shouldering a growing financial burden, and the VA hospital was cost-free.

She phoned the VA Medical Center and was told that no rooms were available. The hospital admitted veterans with service-connected illnesses or injuries first; others—subject to eligibility requirements—if there was room. A patient's financial status and the urgency of his need for care were qualifying factors.

With the help of a neighbor, Amy wrote to her mayor, her councilman, her congressman, enlisted the aid of her minister and both the neurologist and the family doctor handling Andy's care. Officials wrote letters to the medical center, the doctors approved Andy's transfer, the days passed, and the VA responded to Amy as it had from the first: No room.

For five weeks, Andy's therapy continued at Morton Plant Hospital, a non-profit community hospital that now has some 745 acute-care beds, 126 extended-care beds, and continues to grow with southwest Florida since it first opened its doors on New Year's Day in 1916.

Amy's daily visits were mostly in the evenings after work, except on her late days when she didn't finish work until 9:00 p.m. She observed the nurses providing Andy's basic hygiene, and it wasn't long before she became a part of that nightly routine. "I'd stay until visiting hours were over at eight o'clock," she says, "and then I'd get his toothbrush ready and I'd brush his teeth. I'd never done anything like that before in my life except maybe with the children when they were very young. I'd empty the water from the toothbrushing and I'd get a basin of water and wash his face and I'd brush his hair and get him ready for sleep."

Doug also took on a part of Andy's grooming. "Andy wouldn't shave himself at that time," Amy says. "He acted as though he didn't know how. So every so often Doug would shave him. It didn't happen every day, so

Andy always seemed to have a beard. But when it got bad, Doug would shave him clean. Andy was like a baby who had to have everything done for him. A lot of stroke victims can come home in five or six weeks or less. Andy couldn't. His brain damage was so severe that, even though he was making progress, he wasn't mentally alert enough to be brought home."

On her days off, Amy was at Andy's bedside when the therapists worked with him, and she learned from their example.

"He had been so bad that I couldn't believe it when they had him down in physical therapy about two weeks after the stroke," she says. "They had him walking! They had a brace on his leg, and the nurse was supporting him, and he was walking around the room. It was unbelievable."

Because Andy was aphasic, or at least dysphasic, and was so disoriented when he regained full consciousness, speech therapy had started in the ICU and continued to be a major part of his rehabilitation at Morton Plant Hospital.

Andy's vocabulary at this point was limited to "you" and "yes" and "no," and he might say any one of those words in response to any question asked of him. As his visitors had realized, he appeared to understand what was being said to him, yet, as Jim Murphy put it, they wondered whether they were really communicating with him. Certainly he had an expressive problem. Did he also have a receptive one—inability to understand the spoken or written word? It was natural for easygoing, outgoing Andy Robertson to look at the smiling face of a visitor and say "Yes" in answer to questions that, to the questioner, seemed to call for a "Yes" answer.

"Did you sleep well last night?" a visitor might ask.

"Yes," Andy would beam, although he may have spent a very restless night. Or "No" might be the answer even if he slept soundly through the night. Similarly, if a visitor asked if he were feeling better on any given day, Andy might answer "Yes" or "No" without any bearing on the truth of the matter.

Ann Moss, a speech-language pathologist at Morton Plant Hospital, works with patients like Andy Robertson every day, patients who may be trapped inside themselves with their own unspoken thoughts, sometimes listening to what sounds like gibberish. To determine the extent of a patient's problem and to measure his progress, she puts patients through a variety of tests, some of which should be helpful to you if you're trying to determine the degree to which a stroke patient in your family comprehends and to assess his recovery.

Andy's speech therapist, for example, in trying to encourage Andy to point to the parts of his face, was actually testing both his understanding and his visual perception. Did Andy realize that it was his *nose* the therapist wanted him to point to? Was Andy's problem one of locating the parts of his face or of understanding which parts he was being asked to locate? Or both?

On her own initiative, Amy began to reinforce Andy's spatial disorientation therapy. "I'd watch the speech therapist work with him," she says. "She'd tell him to point to his nose, point to his mouth, point to his ears, and he'd point in all the wrong directions. He couldn't identify the parts of his face. After the therapist would leave, I'd feel bad about it. Since I had so many hours to sit there, I started working with him too. I'd try to do the things I'd seen the therapist do. I'd get the same result, and then I'd start over—'Point to your nose, point to your ears.'"

Time would slip by, and suddenly, to her delight, Andy would start following her commands. "I'd go home feeling like I'd really accomplished something," she says. "Then I'd come back the next day, and I'd have to start all over. He wouldn't remember where anything was. In a way it was funny to watch him point off into space, but it also just seemed hopeless."

In Andy's case, the problem was probably twofold at the start—visual perception and ability to understand. But it was by no means hopeless. Within two weeks, he had improved to the point where he was able to feed himself. His urine catheter was also removed during that period, and, since possible urinary tract infections are always associated with such catheters, its removal eliminated one more threat to Andy's recovery.

Although his vocabulary did not immediately increase, his understanding obviously did. "He couldn't write," Romson notes, "but if you put his name in front of him, he was able to copy it. He seemed to be responding to each of the different types of therapy." Amy, too, seemed to be responding to the new responsibilities placed on her. It was not easy, nor is it easy for anyone directly affected by a stroke in the family.

Testing Andy's ability to comprehend went beyond asking him questions that called for a yes or no answer. Andy was asked his name, his address, his birthdate, how long he had lived at his present address.

Therapists also placed a toothbrush, a comb, a fork, and other objects side by side and asked him to point to the toothbrush, for example. How he responded indicated his ability to understand the question. Likewise, a therapist would point to a chair, a window, a door—objects Andy was familiar with in his own environment—and ask him to identify them. Amy sat in on several speech therapy sessions with him at a later stage of his recovery and then was able to repeat the tests and drills that the therapists gave him. They also were able to work together using a workbook that had been provided by a speech therapist.

Moss gives these further examples of language problems and language therapy in her following professional overview of the speech rehabilitation of stroke patients like Andy Robertson:

Auditory discrimination becomes a problem when a patient can't differentiate between the sounds of two words. You point to a utensil and say "Fork." The patient replies "Twarp." He may become angry or frustrated as you repeat the question because he thinks he is saying the word just as you said it to him. Andy had a variation of this problem. Whatever word he said came out clearly, but he may have been thinking "no" and his answer came out "yes," without his realizing or hearing that he'd said the wrong word. For that reason, Moss notes, you can't put too much faith in a stroke patient's yes or no answers until you're sure he or she can discriminate between the two words. Nor can you always trust the inflections a patient puts on a word.

To help a patient with auditory discrimination, therapists may write the two words on separate cards, show him which word he's saying, and stress the differences in pronunciation between the two. If, for instance, he continues to say "twarp" for "fork" and in that way manages to communicate, those around him will understand him and the problem may be overlooked. More likely, however, if he's making that error with one word, he's making it with many, and he probably is not consistent in his mispronunciation. So practice—and patience on the part of his teachers—is important.

Apraxia is a problem that occurs when the brain doesn't feed the proper messages to the mouth even though the oral muscles may be capable of executing the proper order. Early in his recovery, if Andy had been asked to open his mouth, he might have stuck out his tongue instead. Severe apraxia patients are often regarded by therapists as good candidates for communication devices, small machines with tape-recorded messages that the patient can be taught to use by pressing buttons. Or patients may be able to make themselves understood by using gestures, a common practice of Andy's even after he overcame the early apraxia. If he wanted to refer to his mother but couldn't get the word "mother" out, he'd point in the general direction of where his mother lived, Amy says. "It's really a guessing game, and I usually have an idea of what to guess with Andy. I've seen the wives of other stroke patients do the same. I couldn't understand what their husbands were saying, but they could because they understood their husbands." On the most simple level, a patient who wants a drink of water may learn to indicate that by raising his hand to his mouth as though he were drinking from a glass.

Therapist Moss considers apraxic patients as among the most difficult speech cases to work with and says success for them must be measured in terms of percentages. "Everyone wants to be 100 percent recovered," she says, "and sometimes it's very difficult for the patient and his or her spouse to be satisfied with 50 percent. But that may be the patient's limit, and the family has to recognize that half the time the patient may be telling them what he needs and half the time he may not. Accepting that fact will reduce frustration."

Paraphasic errors refer to the substitution by patients of one word or sound for another or the use of senseless combinations of words. Often the patients recognize the error when they make it, but they can't correct it. Andy, for instance, mentally groping for a word, may substitute a word he doesn't mean to say, correct himself by saying "No," and then repeat the wrong word. If given paper and pencil, however, he will be able to write the correct word. But some patients think they've said the right word and don't understand why they aren't being understood. Words that are frequently involved in such errors include "who," "what," "when," and "where."

Perseveration is similar in that the patient may repeat the same word in reference to various objects or in answer to various questions. Show such a patient a set of utensils, for example, and then point to the knife and ask, "What's this?" The patient may pleasantly surprise you by answering "Knife." Then point to the fork and ask, "What's this?" In reply, the patient may repeat "Knife." He may say the same when you point to the spoon. The problem is not that the patient thinks each of these utensils is a knife, but that he either thinks he is saying "fork" and "spoon" or, as Amy notes in Andy's case, "that's the only word that will come out sometimes. He knows it's wrong, but he can't get the right word to come out."

Auditory memory recall is, as the name implies, a reference to the patient's ability to remember objects. Say the therapist shows him not only a knife, fork, and spoon, but a pencil, toothbrush, and so on, ten objects in all. Then to test him the therapist may ask: "Show me the pencil." "Show me the spoon." Once Andy was capable of performing his morning hygienic activities, he soon could identify his toothbrush, hairbrush, razor, and so on. But Amy continued to practice with him using his workbook, which contained pictures, for instance, of objects in series and required him to identify specific ones.

On a more advanced level, a therapist may read a patient a story, perhaps a short article from a newspaper, and then ask him questions about what he's heard. Remember the left hemiplegic discussed earlier who seemed fully recovered but actually had no memory of preceding events? This test would have helped uncover his problem.

Visual perception tests the patient's visual comprehension. Does the visual mechanism of his brain enable him to identify or match two similar pictures? The therapist may show him two series of circles, triangles, crosses, and the like and ask him to match the circles or the crosses. "Sometimes that doesn't have any meaning to the patient whatsoever," Moss says. As part of this visual comprehension testing, she may also check on the patient's own reading comprehension and reading recall. Can he read a newspaper or magazine article, understand what he read, and recall it? Andy's visual comprehension improved so well over the course of his therapy that he was capable of painting a scene that Amy would clip from a newspaper for him to copy. He also resumed reading the newspaper and became interested in looking up words in the dictionary that he had heard in conversation. Amy remembers particularly a sympathy card they sent on the death of a relative. Andy used the dictionary to write the message and to specify some of the things he remembered about their relationship. "It was truly beautiful," Amy says.

The therapist's comprehension test may also extend to short mathematical calculations. One of Amy's big complaints about Andy before he suffered his stroke was that his checkbook was never balanced. Since his stroke recovery, he can balance it to the penny. The reason is certainly not that his stroke improved his mathematical ability. Rather, it is probably that Andy was always capable of doing the necessary math involved but in the past simply didn't regard it as important; it was drudgery. Now it is a challenge, something he considers very important, and that provides a feeling of accomplishment.

Oral encoding is the test of a patient's verbal expression. He is asked to repeat words such as his name, address, and so on. Some patients accomplish this well. Then the test is used to find out if the patient can initiate words through what are called "rote skills"—counting, for instance. That's an automatic process, saying the numbers 1, 2, 3, 4, and so on, without having to stop and think about which number follows next. Andy has no difficulty counting, and, in fact, often has to rely on counting to reach a number he wishes to communicate. If he were asked how many children he has, for instance, he might have to respond "one, two, three, four" because he couldn't say the number 4 alone.

On a higher level of oral encoding tests, Andy can quickly complete such simple sentences as "Open the_____" or "Shut the_____." Again, the response is considered automatic, requiring no processing by the mind.

A speech pathologist, Moss says, generally concentrates on one area or problem of speech and understanding until the patient performs it satisfactorily, as Andy's speech therapist did with his initial problem of spatial disorientation. Once Andy had overcome that problem, the therapist was able to move on to other problems. Andy also illustrates a common characteristic of stroke patients: They can say nouns far more easily than they can say verbs. So Andy can use words like "table," "chair," and "book," but has difficulty when asked what one does with a book. "He uses very few verbs," Amy says, "and no adverbs or prepositions at all. Mostly just nouns."

Syntax, another speech problem, is also one Andy has overcome. A stroke patient might put the words of a sentence in the wrong order because his brain does not give them in proper sequence. "How are you?" might come out instead as "How you are?" or "Are you how?" In the beginning of Andy's recovery, Amy says, "the words would come out backwards." As his recovery progressed, so did his sentence structure—though Andy says very few complete sentences, and those he uses are no more than three or four words.

Prosody is a variation in the rhythm of a stroke patient's speech that appears as a sort of stuttering. Andy sometimes says a word and then makes hesitation sounds—"ah,ah,ah,ah"—until he can get out the next word. Regretfully, therapists often find that some listeners are too impatient to wait—or think they're helping—so they finish a thought for him, causing him further frustration. Such impatience is not to be confused with the kind of assistance a stroke patient might receive from a spouse or close family member when he is struggling to communicate. Amy has become so familiar with Andy's frames of reference, for instance, that she seems almost to read his mind on some occasions, supplying not just a word but the thought that he was unable to express.

Graphic skills are also part of a speech therapist's work, especially teaching the patient to write a legible signature. Here Andy did very well. At first his left-handed signature was weak and shaky, but, after a time, it became strong and precise. In addition, well along in his therapy, his interest in and skill at painting in acrylics began to develop. Amy was always on the lookout for scenes he could copy. Other patients don't necessarily improve to such a degree. "Many aphasic patients can't copy, much less write independently," Moss says, "so they have to be started at a very low level."

Sequence planning is another area in which Andy has recovered well. Actually, it's an extension of speech and language therapy beyond what might be considered its natural boundaries of talking, writing, and understanding. Because stroke patients need and want to function independently, this type of therapy also encompasses teaching the patient to reason, to plan, to perform activities in proper sequence. To boil water for a cup of instant coffee, for example, Andy had to relearn the order in which to proceed— pour water into a pot, put the pot on the stove, turn on the heat—a simple process we take for granted.

Once Andy went home, he would be alone most of the day. So, like patients who live alone, he had to learn how to survive on his own. Some patients who live alone have no idea how to make out a grocery list. They can't think categorically of the items they might need from a store, or, if they could, they couldn't spell the words. They may be able to say and write a few words, but unless their speech or writing is functional, they need help in communication. Although Amy feared the day when she would have to leave Andy home alone, he began to show progress with his hospital therapist in this important area—progress that was to grow in time.

Language therapy today also enlists the aid of many devices, including computers to facilitate re-learning—the communication devices referred to earlier. Speech therapists should be able to help family members of stroke patients become aware of the devices most appropriate to their patient's needs. Some devices, for instance, have prerecorded messages. The patient then learns that if he pushes button A, a voice will advise anyone at his bedside or chairside that he has to go to the bathroom; button B may request a drink of water. One device Andy worked with enabled him to pick out words and phrases on a computer screen or keyboard, and the machine would then read out the completed sentence. Another, a child's learning toy, was programmed to ask the patient to spell out words by pushing letters on a keyboard. Still another came with index-type cards that could be fed into it, triggering the same message written on the card. (Texas Instruments and Bell and Howell are two companies active in this field.) The messages were words and phrases for him to learn—the names of objects around the house such as lamps, chairs, and beds and such expressions as "Close the door" or "Open the window." Amy could even write her own message on a card and record it as well for him to play. Still another device can be hooked up to the telephone to allow an aphasic patient to communicate electronically in writing with the person on the other end of the phone with a similar device.

Can deficits in speech and understanding caused by stroke be improved on? Most health professionals say emphatically yes, and Andy's own progress bears them out. As his brain swelling subsided, some spontaneous recovery occurred, and Amy credits a good deal of his improvement to this automatic recovery—simply the body's healing process. But she also agrees with the therapists who maintain, as Moss puts it, that stimulation of the brain as quickly as possible during recovery leads to further improvement. Although a dead cell cannot be regenerated, many damaged cells can be. Even patients who have appeared to reach a plateau at which their progress has stopped may become capable of performing at a higher level. How long their progress will continue is impossible to forecast.

When there is no regeneration of certain cells, according to Moss, therapists try to focus on another area of the brain. "Supposedly we utilize only about 20 percent of our brain's capacity. So we try to use another area of the brain to serve as closely as possible the function the patient now lacks." Each part of the brain is programmed like a computer to serve certain functions. "If one area of the computer is knocked out," Moss says, "we try to reprogram another area to take over that function. We're pulling from all other areas of the brain to help retrain that area."

In part, the outcome of such efforts is that some stroke victims learn to compensate, learn to use gestures as Andy does, for instance, to supplement limited speech.

Speech therapists often work a good deal with the spouse and family of the stroke patient as well as with the patient. Sometimes, as in Amy and Andy Robertson's case, the spouse voluntarily involves herself in the therapy right at bedside. If the couple has a good relationship, spouse interaction is generally regarded as very helpful. If their relationship has been poor, however, the involvement of the unaffected spouse can be detrimental.

As with auditory discrimination patients, therapists encourage the use of cards or sheets of paper with pictures and words on them to aid in communication. The cards played an integral part in Andy's recovery process. The use of both picture and word together helped him to make an association between the two and stimulated different aspects of his brain. The aim is to integrate and stimulate as many parts of his brain function as possible. Andy's workbook carried similar drills and enabled Amy to work with him throughout his recovery.

As she learned, working with a spouse under such circumstances requires a great deal of patience and perseverance. Questions and comments have to be kept simple, but the answers required have to go beyond yes and no, both to help evaluate a spouse's ability to comprehend and to stimulate his brain. **It can be a frustrating experience for the affected spouse, too, so, Moss warns, never tell him: "I know just how you feel." Whatever your own frustrations, you don't!**

In some cases, direct involvement of a spouse in the learning process may be difficult for the patient. A very independent man who has been head of his household for many years and now can no longer speak may feel degraded to be put through language processing by or in front of his wife. Andy and Amy's closeness seems to have safeguarded them against that problem. "He has always indicated that it hasn't bothered him," Amy says. "He's not embarrassed, and I don't get embarrassed. I feel that I should be helping him if I can. A lot of times, I know exactly what he wants to say, and, if I'm not too busy, I'll make him say it. He'll really try, and he can do it if I can give him the time."

If the patient is too humiliated to have his spouse present or assisting in his therapy, however, Moss recommends that he have sessions alone with the professional therapist and that the therapist then involve both the wife and the husband in a discussion of the affected spouse's progress and prospects. The patient is included in the conference so that he doesn't feel something is being kept from him; the wife is included on the grounds that both have the right to know what the problems are. Often it's difficult for the wife or therapist to judge how much of the discussion the patient understands. But the wife should not take for granted that any of her comments will be missed. Most health professionals can cite instances of even unconscious patients who later recall comments made in their presence.

Generally, speech therapists work with each patient for a half-hour session at Morton Plant Hospital and typically at other hospitals as well. If the patient has been discharged from the hospital and has to travel back for outpatient sessions, the therapy is usually extended to an hour, with a break about halfway through. The therapy sessions are also carefully structured to deal with the various aspects of the recuperative problem and are generally intertwined with the other therapies undertaken with the patient. In some cases a patient may be discharged from the hospital to an intermediate-care facility or a home health program and then referred to the hospital's outpatient program when he has made sufficient progress. Or his doctor may refer him to a therapy center in the community. An advantage of remaining in the hospital's program is that he may be able to visit the same therapists who are already familiar with his needs and his progress.

An adjunct to speech therapy in the community—and one that Amy and Andy have made an important part of their lives—is the stroke club, which will be described in detail in a later chapter. Such clubs provide a meeting forum for stroke patients and their spouses and can be both supportive and inspirational.

N · I · N · E

SOCIAL SERVICE DEPARTMENT BENEFITS

*We fell through the cracks—
too young for Medicare, not poor
enough overall to qualify for
the various assistance programs.*

AMY ROBERTSON

The kind of language therapy program Andy Robertson received at Morton Plant Hospital is the kind stroke patients and their families can expect in any hospital with a strong rehabilitation team. But, as Amy was increasingly becoming aware, rehabilitation costs money. In addition to the daily hospital charges, she now could expect separate charges from each therapy department—speech, occupational, and physical therapy—for the time each therapist spent with Andy.

Today, Morton Plant charges about $25 to $30 for each half-hour of physical or occupational therapy and almost $40 for a half-hour of speech therapy. Its rates are probably within the range of those of most major hospitals, especially those in metropolitan areas, though rates will vary over time and according to both geographic location and the setting in which the services are delivered—inpatient, outpatient, home care, etc. (Therapists and hospitals serving your community are the best sources of local rates. See Appendix.)

Andy was seeing therapists once or twice a day and was now entering his sixth week in the hospital. Where was the money to come from?

Amy carried private health insurance through her employer, but that paid only 80 percent of their costs after a small deductible was met. So she went to the hospital's Social Services Department for advice.

Social services, which is part of the stroke team, meets with stroke patients and/or their families to develop a social history and assessment of the family with a view to discharge planning. There are two aspects to that planning—how well the patient has progressed and the family's financial and personal situation.

Amy's financial situation was dire. Her income—about $100 a week in take-home pay—was their only source of support. Now she and the social services worker would explore other avenues of possible financial assistance.

Medicare was ruled out immediately because Andy was under sixty-five years of age and therefore did not qualify for Medicare benefits. Had Medicare coverage been available to them it would have lightened their financial burden considerably.

Though Medicare's charges to its beneficiaries have been rising, its benefits as of January 1, 1985, call for a deductible of about $400 and then payment of all covered expenses for the first sixty days of a patient's hospitalization. Those covered benefits include laboratory and X-ray services, intensive care, medical supplies and appliances, and such rehabilitation services as speech, physical, and occupational therapy.

In addition, if a patient needs home health care after his hospitalization and his physician arranges for it within fourteen days of his discharge from the hospital, Medicare will continue to pay for the various therapies and the part-time use of skilled nursing care.

Or, if the patient is discharged to a rehabilitation facility or enters one within thirty days of discharge, the program will cover all the same services without charge for the first twenty days and then for about $45 a day for the next eighty days. Emergency room care and outpatient therapies also are covered by Medicare.

Amy herself ruled out the option of simply declaring herself too indigent to pay the bill. "I wasn't that bad off," she says, "especially with the health insurance covering the largest part of it." So, on the advice of the social worker, she called her local Social Security Administration office and made an appointment to explore the avenue of disability benefits.

She was in for a shock. "When I got there, they had all Andy's past employment information ready, and we found on going over it that Andy and I weren't eligible for any disability benefits." Because he'd been self-employed and underemployed or unemployed for most of the preceding eight years, Andy had not paid enough into the program to qualify for benefits.

The sympathetic Social Security employee interviewed Amy at length to see if she might be eligible for some sort of state or county financial assistance. The fact that they owned a home, that both Amy and Andy had a car, their savings, and other assets ruled out any financial help from these sources, too.

"We fell through the cracks—" Amy says, "too young for Medicare, not poor enough overall to qualify for Medicaid or any of the various assistance programs. Sally even went through the process of applying for food stamps, but she was told we didn't qualify economically there either. That was really crushing. I didn't know where to go next."

Meanwhile, the social services member of the stroke team was proceeding with another aspect of her role—determining where the patient goes after he leaves the hospital. To make that decision, she explores with other team members how well he is responding to therapy, whether he can get around with minimal assistance, whether he is making progress in mastering the activities of daily living, what the speech therapist has determined about his ability to communicate.

From spouses or from the patient himself if he's capable, she'll learn what the family can do in terms of caring for him at home, his former employment status, hobbies, interests, anything in his background or the family's background that might be helpful in judging his best placement.

In the past, she'd typically have fifteen to twenty days during which the patient would continue to progress in the hospital—even longer in extraordinary cases like Andy's—and the family would make its initial adjustment and prepare for his return. Now, with the federal accent on reducing covered lengths of stay in the acute-care hospital and with federal guidelines for

Medicare-covered services likely to put pressure on private insurers as well, patients are generally discharged more quickly after a stroke and may be more likely to need a higher degree of post-hospital care than was previously the case.

About this time, the hospital social worker also made Amy aware of the institution's spouse support program, where she could meet with others trying to deal with the same problems. Such programs may show films on stroke, followed by question-and-answer periods during which spouses can clear up their own misconceptions, obtain needed advice, and share common problems.

In addition, **social services can advise families of financial and other assistance available. Unlike Amy and Andy, most families will probably qualify for Social Security disability payments.** In some states, Florida for example, the family can also apply for "state supplemental income," provided they meet the state's residency requirements. Or a family may qualify for Medicaid assistance, depending on their total income and financial status. The indigent may also have the option of seeking assistance through their county's Social Services Department.

On another level, social services can advise families regarding the independent rehabilitation facilities that may be available in their areas and can be used much like the hospital's outpatient department. Some areas have the equivalent of licensed boarding homes for patients who still need twenty-four-hour nursing care but are past the need for treatment in an acute-care hospital. A social services member of the stroke team can advise a family of the cost of these services and help them determine the limits of its health insurance coverage—most of which does not pay for care in an extended-care facility. She can also facilitate arrangements for the patient to receive continued health-care services at home or to return to the hospital for therapy on an outpatient basis. If needed, she will also make nursing home arrangements.

Finally, the social services worker can inform the family of helpful programs in the community—"Meals on Wheels," for example, which might be a major benefit to families like the Robertsons in which no one is at home when the patient needs to be fed. She can also arrange for special equipment—shower stool, bathtub railing, toilet railing—in the home prior to the return of the patient. She might also be able to provide a spouse with a list of volunteer agencies in the community, some of which simply provide volunteers to the home to give a spouse a brief respite to go shopping or visit a friend or have some leisure time. Such respites, whether arranged with organizational help or just through the consideration of friends and relatives, are considered important by those in the stroke field for the rehabilitation of the total stroke family.

Not all hospital social services departments are this complete or this effective, of course, so the family of a stroke victim might consider its first step as the exploration of what its hospital Department has to offer. But regardless of the family's income, insurance, or economic status, it should take advantage of the department's availability.

Unfortunately for Amy and Andy, they fell through those cracks in almost every way imaginable. Ordinarily, if a family can handle the patient at home, he is generally sent there, and Social Services arranges additional therapy after consultation with team members, including his private physician. The physician may order continued therapy at home, and the hospital will coordinate the services, evaluating which therapies the patient needs and contacting the agencies in the community that provide such therapy. Or the patient may be brought several times a week to the hospital for outpatient therapy.

But Amy felt she could not bring Andy home. He was not capable of functioning independently and, since she was now the family's support, she could not be home all day to take care of him. Nor could the Robertson children, all occupied with work or school. Because of her employment, Amy couldn't even take advantage of the spouse support program. She could not afford to keep Andy any longer at Morton Plant Hospital, but she could also not afford to pay for his care in any type of rehabilitation facility. She could come up with only one alternative. Though she hated the thought of taking him from the hospital—where he was progressing so well—she felt their financial survival depended on it, and sweet, mild Amy, with her mother-in-law, Eleanor, as her accomplice, launched a desperate plan.

T · E · N

BREAKING INTO THE VA HOSPITAL

*We really couldn't afford much,
so I tried desperately to get him
into the VA hospital.*

AMY ROBERTSON

The plan had its genesis in the remark of a spokesman at the VA hospital during one of Amy's frequent telephone calls seeking Andy's admission.

She had learned that veterans' hospitals in this country are open without charge to veterans with honorable or general discharges who meet certain eligibility criteria. Priority is given first to veterans seeking treatment for service-connected injuries or illnesses and next to those with service-connected problems who are seeking treatment for other conditions. **But veterans like Andy with non-service-connected illnesses or injuries are also eligible for VA care if their hospitalization is considered necessary by the examining VA physician, if they cannot pay the cost of hospitalization elsewhere, and if beds are available.** Certainly, Amy knew, they qualified under the financial need requirement, but Andy's stroke was not related to his naval service and, already hospitalized and now making recovery, his need for care at the VA facility appeared less than medically urgent. Nor, she had been told time and again, was there a bed available for him.

Nevertheless, Andy's admission was urgent to Amy. How could she work to support the family and be home to take care of Andy at the same time? How could she keep him at Morton Plant Hospital when he had already exceeded the normal length of stay there and when the medical bills were still mounting? Added to that was the fear that those in the stroke field say affects spouses and families of many stroke patients: Can I handle his needs at home?

Amy's mother-in-law also contributed to her concern. "She'd worry about anything that could happen to him," Amy says, "and then I'd start to worry."

The swimming pool at home was part of their concern. Suppose he stumbled while he was home alone and fell into the pool? He could drown. No one would be there to help him. Such thoughts tormented Amy as she considered Andy's difficulty with walking and balance. She continued to press her case through the letters and phone calls to the VA hospital.

Then the comment by the VA spokesman over the phone started her thinking along another line. "He told me that if a patient needing care was brought there, the hospital would accept him, but that at present it would not guarantee that it would take my husband," she says. She mulled over the words in her mind. "If a patient needing care is brought here, we'll accept him. . . ." In other words, she thought, if a patient were taken to the hospital and "abandoned" on its doorstep, the hospital would have to take him in, wouldn't it? Or would it? There was no guarantee.

Amy told her mother-in-law, Eleanor, what she was thinking and found a willing co-conspirator. "I'll even pay for the ambulance," Eleanor told her. "We'll have him picked up and taken there, and we'll just leave him there and see what happens. We'll trust to luck."

They hesitated. Amy tried the VA hospital again. Finally, Amy says,

"We decided that if they didn't call me from the VA hospital by Friday, March 7, we were going to take matters into our own hands." It was no easy decision for a basically mild-mannered wife and a moderately disabled woman of almost seventy to make. But Eleanor was strong, and Amy was growing more aggressive almost by the day. They set their plan in motion in advance, calling a private ambulance company and arranging for an ambulance to meet them in front of the hospital at precisely 10:00 a.m. Friday. They'd call off the plan if the VA hospital came through. But Friday arrived without any word from the VA.

Friday was scheduled to be a very late workday for Amy—she had to report to the store at 5:00 p.m. Eleanor arrived at her home shortly before 10:00 a.m., and they set off together in Eleanor's car for Morton Plant Hospital. The plan called for Amy to ride in the ambulance alongside Andy while Eleanor followed in her car. Once Andy was delivered and accepted, Eleanor would drive her home. From there, Amy would take her own car and go to work. Eleanor was confident; the message for that day in her book of daily prayers was "Prayer changes things." Certainly they had prayed, and she saw the message as an indication that the day would be a good one. Like Amy, her faith in God was strong.

They parked on the hospital grounds and waited at the door. The ambulance failed to arrive by 10:00 a.m. By 10:30 there was still no ambulance, and their agitation was increasing. Part of their scheme had entailed getting Andy released from the hospital before 11:00 a.m. so he wouldn't be charged for another day. It was getting on toward 11:00 when they went upstairs to his room, visited with him, and waited.

Andy had not been told, had no idea that he was to be taken out of the hospital where he'd spent more than five weeks. They planned to keep that from him until the last minute because **at this stage of his recovery he was doing a great deal of crying, as is common among stroke patients.** He cried when anyone entered his room, he cried when anyone left, he cried over anything and over nothing. The longer they could keep from upsetting him, they felt, the better.

The waiting grew more difficult as 11:00 a.m. passed and still no ambulance. No ambulance by noon. Amy went out to the nurses' station on the floor and told the nurses that she was going to take Andy to the VA hospital when the ambulance arrived. They and the doctors knew of her efforts to get him admitted to the veterans' facility. The doctors had approved of a transfer in the past. The nurses made arrangements for Amy to sign Andy out.

Finally, at 1:00 p.m., two ambulance attendants walked into Andy's room. Too many calls that morning, they explained, had tied them up. Amy informed Andy he was leaving. He cried terribly; she felt her resolve slipping. "I don't know if it was his nerves or if he was really that upset and sad about leaving," she says. "It's a terrific hospital. But he cried and cried."

The ambulance attendants rolled their gurney alongside the bed and deftly moved Andy onto it. He stopped crying—until the nurses came into the room to say good-by. Then he burst into tears again. Eventually, the procession emerged from the room—the two attendants pushing Andy on the gurney, Amy and Eleanor walking along as they proceeded to the elevator and then down to the waiting vehicle. Eleanor got into her car and swung in behind the ambulance.

"I wanted to ride in the back with him and try to console him," Amy says, "but I had to ride up front with the driver. The attendant stayed back with Andy." Throughout the trip, as Amy peered through the window behind her seat, the driver maintained a steady stream of communication with the attendant in the rear and the attendant kept checking and reporting Andy's condition. He took his blood pressure, his pulse, made sure he was breathing satisfactorily. Once in the ambulance, Andy stopped crying, and they sped along the familiar roads toward the VA hospital, 15 miles away.

As they arrived at the hospital, Amy's apprehensions grew. They pulled up in front of the door and she stepped from the ambulance and gathered up her courage. A nurse rushed out to meet them, and the attendants started removing Andy. "My husband," Amy said, "he's had a stroke. We just brought him here from Morton Plant Hospital. He needs care."

The nurse didn't delay to ask questions. She summoned help immediately and Andy was rushed inside to the emergency room. Eleanor joined Amy and the ambulance attendants. She handed the attendants a check for about $80 and sat down with Amy in the waiting room. Despite their initial intention to "abandon" Andy, they couldn't leave. The wait was reminiscent to Amy of the one she'd had outside the other emergency room about five weeks earlier when the whole ordeal began. Like that first emergency, it was to drag on for several hours.

Then, as though bearing out the forecast of the daily prayer, a familiar figure walked by, the Reverend Morton, whose church they attended. When he spotted Amy and Eleanor, he stopped to talk. Amy told him what they'd done and their reasons for doing it. "I also told him we didn't know what was going on, that we'd been there for hours, that no one had talked to us, that we didn't even know if they were going to keep him."

The minister assured them he'd find out. He walked into the ER, and for a time it seemed to Amy and Eleanor that he, too, had been swallowed up by the big hospital. Finally, he brought them the news they'd been waiting to hear:

"They're going to keep him," he said.

The afternoon dragged on, and Eleanor had to leave. Amy stayed on alone. In the back of her mind was her concern for getting to work by 5:00 p.m. She had no transportation now, but as in so many instances in the Robertsons' battle with stroke, she trusted that God or good fortune would see her through each crisis. She was never wrong.

After she got home, Eleanor telephoned Amy's house and told Doug and Sally that the transfer had been made. "You'd better get down to that hospital," she said. "Your mother is there all alone, and she needs you."

Perhaps it was the strain or the urgency in her voice or the fact that Doug and Sally now knew that their father was back in another emergency room, but they assumed the worst. They ran to Doug's car and sped out of the driveway, determined to cover the miles as quickly as possible. "Doug was driving like a racing driver," Sally recalls, "and we went through every red light on the way there. It was late afternoon, and traffic was already getting heavy. We zigzagged in and out of it."

Doug shifted from gear to gear as he swung around cars and zipped around corners. At one point Sally felt her heart leap to her mouth as her brother swung into the lane for oncoming traffic, sped past three cars stopped at a traffic signal, and zoomed through the stoplight at an intersection. He switched to a potholed back road to avoid some of the traffic and bounced and jounced them over it until at last he pulled up before the hospital. They rushed in to find Amy waiting there quietly.

Andy was moved out of the emergency room and upstairs to a bed in a large ward. Amy and her children were directed to his bedside, and the Reverend Morton joined them. A curtain was drawn around Andy's bed, which was in the corner of the room, no windows around him. Both his bed and the table beside him showed signs of age. The walls were a pale green, and the patient in the bed next to him was very old and unconscious. "It was terrible," Amy says. "It looked like a prison, old drapes, old shades. Morton Plant is a beautiful hospital. Our first view of this one was awful. It broke my heart. I cried when I saw it, and I didn't want to leave him there."

She felt she had no choice. She and the children and their minister stood at the foot of the bed and looked at Andy in the big, bare, green room. The trauma of the flight from Morton Plant and the wild ride had taken its toll on the family. Amy wept. The children stood silently. Eventually, Amy left the children at Andy's bedside, and she and the Reverend Morton made their way past bed after bed until they were out of the ward and then out of the hospital. They got into the minister's car. Amy still had to be at work by 5:00 p.m. The Reverend Morton drove her there.

She arrived at work shortly after 5:00 and asked for permission to go out for a hamburger and bring it back to eat in the stockroom. Her manager was shocked to learn that, except for a candy bar, she had eaten nothing all day. "He told me to take a break and go eat in the lounge," she says. "He was so concerned, it was a relief."

When Marv Chester, Andy's real estate associate, went to visit Andy that night at Morton Plant Hospital, he was dismayed to find another patient in Andy's bed.

E · L · E · V · E · N

THE FAMILY COPES AT HOME

The children sort of brought themselves up after Andy's stroke.

AMY ROBERTSON

T he VA Medical Center took on a new look a few days later when, the tension of Andy's transfer over, Sally went to visit her father. Andy had already been moved to another wing, and Sally was greatly relieved by what she saw: The room was bright and airy, with far fewer beds and much cheerier decor. The previous weekend's accommodation had been in the general medicine unit where all stroke patients had to be placed until they could be evaluated for rehabilitation. The new quarters had an immediate effect on Andy's demeanor and outlook, too. He was once again cheerful and happy, with no sign of crying.

Amy also got a different and far better perspective when she returned for a visit that day—a view of VA medical care that she still holds. "First," she says, "we were greatly relieved that they took him in at all. Then, despite the appearances of that first night, he got excellent care. Everything was done for him that had to be done. The people working there were just beautiful people. He got personalized attention; he and the other patients were treated like VIPs."

Just as Amy had visited Andy every day possible at Morton Plant Hospital, so she began her daily visits to his new treatment home at Bay Pines, except on her two late working days. Andy's children also spent a lot of time at his bedside. Financially, Amy could also breathe more easily since there would be no further charges for Andy's hospitalization. But life at home had changed significantly and would never be the same again.

Amy was working forty hours a week. She'd ordinarily start at 9:00 a.m. and finish at 5:00 p.m. Then she'd get into her car and head for the hospital. On the way she'd stop at a fast food restaurant, pick up a hamburger to go, and eat it as she drove. She'd arrive nightly about 5:15 while Andy was having dinner. Sometimes a considerate volunteer worker who was pouring coffee for patients would pour a cup for her; sometimes she drank Andy's while he drank his container of milk.

Visiting hours ended about 8:00, and Amy would usually arrive home by 8:30. Her children had always eaten by then, but they usually saved some dinner for her. They'd also washed their dishes or stacked them in the dishwasher. Susie would be doing her homework, Sally perhaps watching television, Doug out with friends.

"The five of us didn't get together very often," Amy says. "The children sort of brought themselves up after Andy's stroke, and I didn't have much of a life at that time. There was no social life." Frequently she found herself heating some leftovers for her dinner when she got home and then going early to bed.

Nor did they discuss their feelings about Andy's stroke with each other very often. "Mostly," Amy says, "the children kept their feelings to themselves, and I did, too. I didn't want to add to their problems. We tried to be as normal as possible."

Amy's optimistic philosophy also had a major bearing on the family's adjustment to Andy's stroke. "I felt confident that Andy was going to be 100 percent OK in a year, and I told that to the children many times, especially at first," she says. "I'd say it takes a long time for a person to get over a stroke, but we're in no hurry. We'll just take our time, and Daddy will be fine. I guess I convinced them of that, and we didn't make too much of the situation. We lived one day at a time. That was all we could do. As time went by, I just forgot about any timetable for his recovery, and they just accepted things as they were. They never brought it up. You get used to being in a situation, and it becomes a normal way of life. We didn't dwell on the fact that Andy was in the hospital." She did note, however, that Doug found hospital visits particularly depressing to him and, like Sally earlier, often had difficulty forcing himself to go.

Without Amy home much of the time, family life changed appreciably in many ways. "Sally was more than my right arm," Amy says. "She got me through it. If I wasn't able to do something, she'd just take over and do it. She really kept the house together. She has a way of seeing things that need to be done and then doing them. She was also working from 7:00 a.m. to 3:00, but that job wasn't much of a challenge to her. Maybe that's why the responsibility at home came so easy to her." Sally was also the one Amy spoke with when she did want to talk about Andy.

The children were already used to getting their own breakfasts. "Before I started working, I felt it was my duty to get their breakfasts," Amy says. "Afterward, as the children got older, they became more independent and took care of themselves in the mornings." Lunch, of course, was eaten away from home, and Sally frequently started dinner preparations for Doug, Susie, and herself when she got home from work. Sally also pitched in to assist with the food shopping as well as with the cooking. "I used to do some organizing of what we needed and leave things for them to cook," Amy says. "Then on my days off I'd try to have a good meal for them. But we didn't eat any fancy dinners. It was just too much for me at the time."

Instead of trying to do housework when she got home at night, Amy saved that for her days off. On those days she'd visit with Andy in the afternoon and get home earlier. "I didn't try to do everything," she says. "I'd just do the little things that had to be done in the house, the most important things, and let the rest go. The kids would do the laundry and take care of their own rooms. Except Susie: Her room would go six months without being touched; there were aisles of clothes in it you could walk through. I just left it. I thought, 'Someday she'll grow up and clean her room.'"

Life without Andy at home never got easy. But after a while Amy felt as though she'd been following the same household routine for years. She never knew which days she'd have off from work until she received her schedule the preceding week. Sometimes she'd have to work on the weekend. But, overall, she felt the frequent rescheduling worked to her advantage. If she wanted a specific day off, she could always arrange to have it. She could also be available at various times during the week when her presence might be more in demand at home or at the hospital.

That demand came often; as every stroke family knows, life's problems arise without regard to those a family might already be experiencing. Amy's mother was in failing health, had severe arthritis, and was being cared for by Amy's father at home. He was reluctant to hospitalize her for medical care, but, a few weeks after Andy was admitted to the VA Medical Center, the hospitalization became necessary. Amy and her father discussed the problem at length and then arranged for her mother to be admitted to Morton Plant Hospital.

The following day, as she was driving to work, Amy saw an emergency vehicle, its siren wailing, speed past her down the street on which her parents lived. Knowing that her mother was already hospitalized, she gave it little thought—until she got to work. Her co-workers delivered the message: "They just took your dad to the hospital. They couldn't reach your son Doug, so they decided on their own to take him. He fell out of a grapefruit tree and broke a lot of bones."

Amy was stunned. "Who are 'they' and where is my son?" she asked.

"They" was the emergency squad, which had telephoned her home to advise someone in the family of the accident but had been unable to get an answer. "I panicked," Amy said, "not only because of my father, but I'd just left Doug sleeping at home, and now I thought something had happened to him, too." When she regained her composure, she quickly checked on both her father and her son. Her father had a fractured pelvis, leg, and finger; her son had slept through the excitement.

Later Amy visited her father at Morton Plant Hospital and learned that he had been picking grapefruit that morning, lost his balance, and fell out of the tree to the ground. Despite his multiple injuries, his condition was not critical. After seeing him, she was able to go upstairs and visit her mother on another floor. She also managed to get in a visit with Andy at the VA Medical Center.

That became her routine for the next two weeks. She'd drive to the VA facility from work, visit with Andy, then drive back to Morton Plant Hospital and see her parents. Some nights she'd bring her mother down to visit her father. "My dad recovered remarkably; it was unbelievable that he could heal so quickly. In two weeks, on the same day, both my mother and father were released from the hospital, and I brought them home to my house. It seemed as though I hadn't been home myself in weeks. We put my parents up in my bedroom, and I moved into one of the children's rooms. Sally was out of work at that time, and my parents paid her to take care of them.

But my dad just couldn't wait to get home. They stayed a week, and then returned to their own home on a Saturday. The next day, Doug was admitted to Morton Plant Hospital for a hernia operation. It had become necessary during that previous week."

Financial survival was also a major concern. Amy never tried to sit down and figure out a plan. "I couldn't," she says. "I didn't have anything to plan with. We lived from paycheck to paycheck."

Andy had been bringing home no money at the time he suffered the stroke, having just associated with Marv Chester's real estate firm, so family finances were in bad shape from the start. "It was a good thing I was working," Amy says, "because most of the time all we were bringing in was what I was making."

She decided not to ask the children for board money or financial assistance. Susie, of course, was still in high school, and Donald was away at college where, fortunately, he had the GI Bill to help pay his educational expenses. Except for the brief period when she was unemployed, Sally contributed board money anyway, and Doug took over Andy's role of maintaining the house and yard, making any needed repairs, and paying any costs himself out of his own earnings. "He could also see things that had to be done without being told, and he'd go ahead and do them. He felt the responsibility of head of the household, and when my car gave me mechanical trouble—as it often did—or when anything else went wrong, he fixed it."

Amy also began to rely on both her sons for advice, and she found their judgment good. She consulted them, for instance, when she began to think about selling Andy's car, partly because she could use the money and partly because she felt he would have no further use for it. "Important things like that," she says, "I always discussed with the boys. They helped me make the decisions."

With their agreement, and without informing Andy because she was afraid it would upset him, she sold the car. She would tell him later, she felt, and meanwhile, "it was a relief not to have the expense of it anymore." Not only did she need the money for support, but, with Andy now in the VA Medical Center, she was ready to deal with the health-care costs of his stay at Morton Plant. She'd put off completing the various insurance forms until his discharge, and now she handled all the paper work at once. That gave her a fix on the 20 percent coinsurance she had to pay.

Mortgage payments on the house also had to be made. They amounted to about $200 a month, but with her take-home pay at about $100 a week, they were not easy to meet. Still, the mortgage had been necessary three years earlier to keep them from losing 22 acres of commercial property they still owned near Detroit. Of the $25,000 mortgage, $16,000 went to pay for the property. Amy gave no thought to selling the property now because the area in which it was located had deteriorated considerably since the purchase. The best she could do, she felt, was get their investment back. "That's been our luck," she says. Instead, she decided to hold on to the land "until maybe something starts booming up there." Payment of debts incurred in Andy's business ventures ate up the rest of the mortgage money.

Many times, especially during those early weeks and months of Andy's hospitalization, Amy had to fight down the feeling of panic. "Once—it must have been the day before payday—I had only 85 cents. I needed bread and I needed milk, and I couldn't decide what to do; I didn't have enough to buy both. Then I got an idea. I started hunting around the house for empty bottles, and I raised 60 cents more, enough to buy both the milk and the bread. I won't forget that. That was the worst time. I never let the children know. All the other times, we managed; it didn't get that low."

Susie's graduation from high school was one of the milestones the family passed while Andy lay in the hospital. Amy's brother-in-law took her to the graduation ceremony. "We considered picking up Andy and taking him," Amy says, "but we decided against it. He hadn't been out to anything since his hospitalization, and we didn't think he was well enough to start with a crowded graduation ceremony." After the graduation, they picked up Amy's sister and Sally, and the four went out to lunch. "I don't think Andy was really aware of events like this," Amy says. "I felt sorry for him because he was missing them.

"When Donald graduated from college, it was the same thing. We didn't feel Andy was up to that, either. So Doug and Donald and their buddy and I went to the graduation, and then I took them all out for pizza and beer. I asked the boys first whether they thought Andy would be able to take it, and they felt it would be too difficult for him and for everybody because he was still in a wheelchair at Bay Pines and it would be a long ceremony and he wasn't ready yet for the crowds."

Graduation ceremony or not, Amy visited Andy those evenings and brought him the news of his family's progress. What she didn't tell him immediately, though, was that Susie's graduation was signaling another major change in the family's life: Susie had decided to get an apartment and move out on her own. Amy was reluctant to let her go and tried to talk her out of it, but Susie had made up her mind.

Susie was a go-getter who would work seven days a week if she felt it was worthwhile. She was already operating a lawn-cutting business and, once on her own, was able to apply for federal assistance to attend a two-year technical college where she could study horticulture. So the Robertson family at home was now down to three, although Susie stayed in close touch.

Amy and the children lived very much in the present in those days, and she avoided thinking about the future. "I couldn't even think about tomorrow because I just had to concentrate on today," she says. "That's how we did it, one day at a time. We'd get through one day, and then we'd get through another day. All I told myself about the future was that it would be better, that Andy was getting better."

Perhaps what sustained her most during this bleak period was the strength she drew from her religion. "I learned from listening to the Reverend Morton's sermons to have faith," she says. "That's the most important thing. And I do have faith. I'm not really a religious person, but a lot of the things he said sank in. Every night when I say my prayers I thank the Lord for letting us live in this house another day because I can't believe we are still here. There were times when we were so close to being out of it. I didn't know how we were going to make it through another month. And we're still here. Every once in a while, when we're in need of it most, somebody comes through or something will happen and we'll come into some money. Not too much, but enough to get us through, and we can live comfortably. Because we are comfortable; we're not hungry. So I just try to keep my faith up."

T·W·E·L·V·E

THE REHABILITATION PROCESS

The goal is to rehabilitate the patient to the fullest extent of his abilities.

DR. D. ROGERS SMITH
Chief of Rehabilitation Medicine
VA Medical Center
Bay Pines, Florida

REHABILITATION NURSING

PHYSICAL THERAPY

CORRECTIVE THERAPY

OCCUPATIONAL THERAPY

The Veterans Administration Medical Center at Bay Pines, Florida, one of more than 170 VA medical centers in the country, resembled a huge resort-hotel complex to Amy Robertson, the kind of place she and Andy might have taken the family for a holiday. The sprawling facility of more than thirty attractive, Spanish-style buildings is spread over 337 well-landscaped acres, with a magnificent view of Boca Ciega Bay and Treasure Island across the water. It has grown from five buildings with 159 hospital beds and 350 domiciliary beds—living quarters for veterans too disabled to care for themselves—when it opened in 1933 to house more than 1,100 beds including a two-building nursing home, a new hospital complete with rehabilitation unit, a new 200-bed domiciliary, and a housing unit for psychiatric patients. A $110 million construction project continues to expand and modernize its units.

Many of the buildings are mid-rises of three to five floors made of poured concrete with stuccoed walls, red tile roofs, screened porches with wrought-iron railings, patios, breezeways, and wide stone steps. Covered walkways connect buildings across green lawns shaded with oak and pine and magnolia, and large, bright rooms look out on courtyards with benches and grassy gardens and a wooden pier that juts out into the bay. A national cemetery on its grounds holds the graves of 4,200 veterans who served as far back as the Indian Wars. And in its units, some 1,700 employees and 1,100 volunteers tend the needs of a patient population drawn from 190,000 eligible veterans from the ten-county area the medical center serves.

The bed to which Andy was admitted that first night was in the general medicine and surgery unit that dated back to the 1930s and has since been extensively renovated for other use, even its faded green walls succumbing to the painter's brush. On March 11, four days later, he underwent an extensive evaluation by rehabilitation therapist Bruce K. Martin, who is now the rehabilitation medicine coordinator at the medical center.

Andy had been responding well to therapy at Morton Plant Hospital, and Martin found him alert, cooperative, and motivated. Though his balance was off, Andy could ambulate 120 feet using parallel bars for support and under close supervision. His passive range of motion—the range in which Martin could manipulate Andy's arms and legs—was found to be normal. He could stand and sit, his general strength and exercise tolerance were fair, and he understood and followed instructions.

Martin signed him up for corrective and occupational therapy immediately, as medically prescribed, and had him moved that day to a rehabilitation unit bed. Physical therapy was begun shortly afterward and by the end of the month speech therapy was started again.

Dr. D. Rogers Smith, currently chief of the Rehabilitation Medicine Service at the VA Medical Center, notes that the essential aim of the program—and of any stroke rehabilitation program—is to rehabilitate the patient to the fullest extent of his abilities. To do that, the medical center not only has state-of-the-art equipment but computers to integrate that equipment and provide readouts that pinpoint patient strengths and weaknesses. In addition to the parallel bars, the walkers, and other aids in ambulation, Dr. Smith says, it has a full range of the most advanced—as well as the traditional—exercise equipment, hydrotherapy, and biofeedback. Therapists use videotape to evaluate treatment and progress and use various aids to occupational, vocational, and physical progress, including a kitchen in which patients may be evaluated and instructed in household skills.

The transfer and all its ramifications appeared to Amy to have set Andy's recovery back a bit. Where he had been more actively on his feet during his last days at Morton Plant Hospital, now in his first days at the VA facility he was more dependent on his wheelchair. Still, therapists in the stroke field readily acknowledge that stroke patients can be expected to have good days and bad days and that some backsliding can be expected from time to time in the best of patients. Amy often wheeled Andy outside, where they could enjoy the sunshine and the view from the hospital grounds. She learned to let his recovery proceed apace. "He was so brain-damaged, so off mentally," Amy says, "that he was really like a baby. A lot of stroke victims come home within six weeks, but I couldn't have taken Andy home at that time. He had to have everything done for him. Orderlies even had to help him into the bathroom and help him shower."

Amy was busy handling administrative matters, too. One of her co-workers had suggested she contact a representative of a veterans' organization about her financial plight, but before she could, an American Legion representative at the Medical Center's Veterans' Affairs Office visited Andy and then telephoned her. Andy's aphasia had made communication on such a difficult subject, especially with a stranger, impossible, so Amy again became the family's voice—a role she was finding increasingly natural though never one she preferred. She met with the Legion official and offered her family's financial status in detail. Completion of forms and a follow-up investigation of the family's economic situation took about a month. When it was over, the news Amy received was almost too good: Because Andy had no income prior to his stroke, no Social Security or other disability benefits, and no prospects at that point of earning an income, and taking the level of Amy's income into consideration, Andy would be eligible for a VA special monthly pension to meet his need for regular "aid and attendance." The pension check of $200 a month started while he was hospitalized. To Amy, it wasn't just a pension, "it was a lifesaver."

Meanwhile, Andy's therapy was proceeding on several fronts. The long-term rehabilitation that he received at the VA Medical Center far exceeds the usual length and degree of rehabilitation given to or even available to stroke patients. Nevertheless, his rehabilitation process will familiarize you with the types of ongoing care important to a stroke patient's recovery—whether that care be given in a general hospital, a rehabilitation hospital or other longer-term facility, or through continuing outpatient care or home services. You have been introduced earlier in this book to the stroke team. Now, as we did with the speech therapist, let's look in more detail at how various other key members of the stroke team were instrumental in Andy's rehabilitation and at their programs for stroke patients, spouses, and families.

REHABILITATION NURSING

"Nurses," says Amy Robertson, "are saints. Doctors have more education, but nurses have more kindness in them."

Amy's regard for nurses grew over the many months of Andy's care, starting in Morton Plant Hospital and extending to his care at the VA Medical Center.

"I used to talk with the nurses when they were at their station," she says, "and I always felt they were so busy I didn't want to say too much to them. But they were always kind, and they'd get me anything I needed to help Andy with bathing, and we'd talk about such things as swimming as therapy when he got home."

From watching them work, she could also see that there are two levels of nurses involved in rehabilitation care. The clinical nurse specialist, who holds a master's degree in rehabilitation nursing, devises and sets up educational and counseling programs. She also evaluates the patient's response to many of the therapy programs and provides not only patient care but consultation for the staff nurses in the rehabilitation unit. The staff rehabilitation nurses work with the patients like Andy on a day-to-day basis and are the primary contact for most patients in the rehabilitation service.

In Andy's room, a staff rehabilitation nurse might help him practice the skills he was learning in the various therapies. "The nurses reinforce the patients' skills in dressing, undressing, hygiene, and so on, that they learn from the occupational therapist, for example," says Loria F. Menousek, a clinical nurse specialist in rehabilitation nursing at the VA Medical Center. "If there's no follow-through on the nursing units, the patients are not going to pick up or use the skills."

Bowel and bladder training also is the province of the rehabilitation nurse as well as of nurses in general. Because of his one-sided paralysis, Andy could have experienced problems in this area, and the problems could have been considerable in that they might also have limited his social interactions. "Stroke patients still have the sensation or the urge to go," nurse Menousek says, "but it's a different sensation than they had before their strokes." An even greater problem in that regard can be the patient's level of consciousness or confusion, including his inability to interpret the sensations he feels. This problem is often more severe in older patients and can be related to the effects of the stroke and to the medication the patient is receiving.

The patient's need to communicate is a complicating factor in bowel and bladder training as well. Andy was an aphasic patient and therefore had to learn how to indicate to his caregivers that he wanted to use the bathroom. His disability also meant he needed assistance in getting there. Because such a patient's awareness that he needs to use the bathroom might be sudden, this can be a problem both for the family caring for him at home and for the professionals working with him in the hospital. It may require speedy communication and the immediate availability of assistance. Nursing intervention in the hospital is aimed at training a patient like Andy to improve his mobility, control, timing, and interpretation and can generally help both in the hospital and later, when the spouse or family takes over his care.

Counseling the spouse is another special activity of the rehabilitation nurse, with the clinical nurse specialist called in for consultation or assistance in the more complex situations. Because of her broader role in the patient's recovery, the specialist usually has more time than the staff rehabilitation nurse to sit down with a spouse and listen to his or her concerns; the staff nurse might be caring for many patients at the same time and under more pressure to meet their immediate needs.

Amy's fear of taking Andy home is a familiar problem to the rehabilitation staff nurse—and one that spouses and families should use her assistance to overcome. Amy didn't. Partly, her job prevented her from being at the medical center during the day, when she might have arranged counseling sessions. But her natural reticence to ask questions and to intrude on the professionals as they went about their duties were also factors.

Ordinarily, to cope with spouses' fears that they won't be able to care for the stroke victim properly at home, Menousek discusses with them the skills they will need, provides them with pamphlets dealing with stroke and stroke rehabilitation, and determines how the hospital can complement the work of the spouse at home. She advises spouses regarding what resources are available to them in the community and may refer them to other members of the rehabilitation team, such as the social worker or any of the various therapists.

Menousek cites one case in which the wife of a stroke patient returned to her with many parts of a booklet on stroke underlined and with questions written in the margins. "I could sit down with her and answer her questions or refer her to someone who would be more appropriate to counsel her in specific areas in which she needed help. I was also able to integrate her into the therapy regimen with her husband so she could learn from his therapists how to reinforce at home what he had learned in the hospital—without taking over for him. It's important that the patient be as independent as possible, but many times his spouse will have to remind him of things."

There are bound to be varying degrees of spouse participation in the caregiving relationship, depending both on the spouse and on the relationship of the couple before the stroke. Not every spouse falls naturally into the role of caregiver, nor does counseling always allay all fears. Caring for a recovering stroke patient is a big responsibility, and in some cases the patient has to be fairly independent before his spouse can handle home therapy. That's why discharge planning is also so important, determining whether the patient is ready to come home, the home is ready to receive him, or some further care in an extended-care facility or nursing home is required.

As Amy's case illustrates, and as is still the case in many hospitals, counseling of stroke patients and their families is on an individual basis and is often a hit-or-miss proposition. However, the VA Medical Center where Andy got his care, among others, is developing an interdisciplinary educational program in which the social worker, dietitian, doctors, nurses, therapists, psychologists, and so on, present a series of classes at which patients and spouses or families are given short presentations and then are encouraged to ask questions. The program will also establish contacts between families and therapists to facilitate discussion of matters that concern the families. The VA program will also provide speakers for stroke clubs in the community to offer further information after the patient has moved home. Unfortunately, spouses like Amy Robertson, who have difficulty getting time off from work to attend the afternoon sessions of such a program, will still have to take the initiative in seeking counseling.

Menousek, who holds a master's degree in rehabilitation nursing and has been working with stroke patients since 1966, notes that attitudes toward stroke as well as the means for treating stroke patients are changing. "The longer life spans people now enjoy and the growing interest in gerontology have spurred interest in stroke because stroke is so often an affliction of the elderly," she says. "For the first time, there is growing recognition in the health-care field that twenty years from now much of the population will be over sixty-five, and we had better learn to deal with this problem." As a result, she feels that **opportunities for rehabilitation of disorders associated with age, including stroke, are better now than they were just five or ten years ago** and that they will continue to improve.

"Stroke patients used to die of pneumonia and urinary tract infections," she says, "but this type of situation is declining. Changes in nursing practice are part of the reason—mobilizing the patients, changing their positions in the bed, getting them out of bed, and in general taking a more active nursing role aimed at rehabilitation. There's a greater respect for and awareness of the health-care needs of the elderly today. More doctors and nurses realize that the elderly are living longer and have special needs."

Menousek also points out that the last major medical system to advance was coronary care, with dramatic results in the resuscitation of heart patients. She believes attention will focus next on the neurological system—a belief current research appears to support. "We are learning more and more about the brain and its functions," she says, "and that knowledge will continue to improve. Preventive stroke research is continuing; new drugs in the field of nuclear medicine may be able to demonstrate problems before brain damage occurs by identifying impaired circulation areas."

In addition, she cites the development of the more sophisticated scanning technologies today for the assessment of stroke damage in the brain and the development of new equipment for improving post-stroke rehabilitation, all of which show promise of brightening the stroke picture.

Like all stroke nurses, physicians, and therapists, however, she puts great emphasis on the importance of both patient motivation and family support in the recovery process. "With almost any stroke patient," she says, "you can't say definitely what he will or won't be able to achieve. If you tell him he'll never walk, he'll never try." Therapists find it better to say to him: "What do you want to do? We'll work with you toward your goal. We don't know how far we're going to get, but we'll certainly help you get as far as you can."

The support of family members in such circumstances, therefore, is tremendously important. Throughout his ordeal, Andy was increasingly aware of Amy's support and of the concern and encouragement of his children. He drew strength and motivation from them, and he also became aware of less fortunate stroke victims, whose families were less attentive. That awareness led to his greater admiration of his own wife and children and provided extra incentive for improving. The family reinforced his own efforts and those of his professional therapists. Because of the value of such a role by the family, the rehabilitation nurse and the nurse specialist, like the other members of the stroke team, make every effort to integrate the family into the patient's recovery process.

PHYSICAL THERAPY

Rehabilitation coordinator Bruce Martin defines **physical therapy, in short, as muscle re-education.** As indicated earlier, it is one of the primary therapies given to a stroke patient, is begun within seventy-two hours of a stroke patient's admission if his medical condition allows, and often continues on an outpatient basis after his discharge from the hospital as long as therapists feel further progress is possible for the patient.

"That doesn't necessarily mean that the patient will be able to get up and walk again," says Kathleen Aadahl, acting chief of physical therapy at the VA facility. "It might mean he'll have to remain at the wheelchair level, but we want to get him to the point where we can say: 'He functions to the best of his ability.'"

Andy's physical rehabilitation, begun in Morton Plant Hospital, was continued in earnest after his admission to the VA Medical Center and throughout the length of his stay. A strong rapport developed between him and the head of physical therapy in one of the several units in which he was quartered, and her concern extended to Amy as well. "She acted as though he was so important to her, and she was so concerned about him," Amy says. "She had a good sense of humor, and she was just perfect to motivate him. He liked her, and he cooperated with her. She also showed me all the equipment he was using in physical therapy and let me observe while he was using it."

Evaluation: Before putting Andy on an exercise schedule, the physical therapist evaluated whether Andy could sit, stand, feed himself, how much total care he was going to need. Therapists have found that some patients tend to lie back after a stroke and not contribute to their own recovery; the therapists and the team must then stimulate the patient's interest in helping himself. Within the first few weeks of working with a patient, the physical therapist has a good idea of the patient's rehabilitation potential. It was as a result of the potential he showed from the time he was admitted that Andy was transferred to the rehabilitation unit. But his motivation flagged from time to time, and it was Amy and the therapists who had to revive it.

Andy's evaluation process was typical of that given to stroke patients. Trunk stability is tested in bed—can he roll, arch his back, extend his limbs? What are his initial functional levels? As he advances, the therapist evaluates whether he can perform wheelchair functions and transfer from wheelchair to bed or bed to wheelchair. In addition, his ability to walk is evaluated, and the therapist recommends whether or when he is able to proceed from walking with the support of parallel bars to using a walker or crutches or a cane.

There is much overlapping and unity among the various therapies because each is a reinforcing process for the others. So in bringing a patient to his maximum functional level, the therapists' aim is to rehabilitate him not only physically but socially, emotionally, and, if possible, vocationally— all of these aspects intricately bound up in each of the therapies that are pursued.

Initial rehabilitation, as noted previously, started for Andy right in the

ICU, with the nurses exercising his limbs even before he regained consciousness. Now the therapist, in moving Andy's arms and legs, was assuming a leading role in preventing the tightening of Andy's muscles, the stiffening of his joints, bedsores, and other complications including possible cardiac and pulmonary troubles. "Virtually every organ in the body can deteriorate fast from undue bed rest," Dr. Smith says. "You have to get the patient active as soon as possible."

The passive physical therapy, that is, the therapist exercising Andy's limbs for him, is also important because lack of physical activity, infrequent turning in bed, weak or ineffective cough, and inhaling of material down the throat are also common causes of atelectasis—the collapse or incomplete expansion of a lung. The therapy also helps prevent thrombosis, which may occur in a paralyzed or weak leg (and which may also require anticoagulant therapy).

Physical therapy techniques include electrical as well as manual stimulation. The therapists may use such agents as ice, water, moist heat, brushing, and biofeedback. Because stroke patients suffer intellectual as well as physical impairment, the "pathway" between the brain and a limb may be interrupted. Through biofeedback, therapists may attempt to bridge that gap and restore needed communication. Newer muscle-training devices have also been introduced that can evaluate weakness in the patient's limb even while he exercises to strengthen that limb.

Working in conjunction with the occupational therapist, the physical therapist also tailors his or her care to problems of depth perception or other visual defects that might affect the patient's walking ability, spatial and other problems of left hemiplegia, or even whether the patient needs more stress placed on his upper extremities.

At the initial planning sessions, therapist Aadahl says, the multi-disciplinary team determines how soon to involve the family in the patient's care and orient the family to whether the patient will be discharged to his home or to a nursing home, for instance. The Bay Pines VA facility is affiliated with about forty nursing homes to which it can transfer veterans in need of further care.

Amy's introduction to physical therapy was minimal because of her unavailability due to employment, but at least she was acquainted with some of Andy's exercises. The therapists prefer to work with the family, Aadahl says. "We have the family with us as we walk the patient, and we have a spouse or other family member exercise the patient, with us there for guidance. Fear is a great deal of what we have to combat—not only the patient's initial fear but the family's fear of the new situation. Families don't know if they can handle it. So we encourage the family to come in, and we encourage them to take the patient home at some point for a day or a weekend, look at the problems they encounter, and then tell us in what areas they need help. We have a checklist for them to take along, and when they bring back the patient, they can feed their problems back to us."

Motivating a patient, as, for instance, when Andy's interest waned, can require the efforts of a supersalesperson in physical therapy. Aadahl cites the case of an eighty-four-year-old man who could not walk or talk, had a urine catheter, and was being treated like a child by his family because he had been mentally devastated by his stroke. To motivate that patient and redirect that family took a super sales effort. The case also illustrates why the sooner a therapist begins to work with a patient, the easier the motivation and rehabilitation process becomes.

Aadahl finds that most spouses are like Amy Robertson—frightened to accept their caregiver roles but receptive to them nonetheless, and hungry for information. "Any reluctance we encounter is usually due to fear of the unknown," she says. "If we can provide patient and family education, the fear pretty much is resolved and the family loses its reluctance."

She agrees with others in the stroke field that physicians don't always have the time to sit down and discuss the stroke situation in detail with the family. Moreover, she notes that families are often reluctant to put their questions to physicians. "Families are usually a little more open with us," she adds. "We're looking at the whole person, not just the involved part, and we're trying to rehabilitate the patient physically, emotionally, sexually, and economically as well."

One of the educational processes she feels will be of assistance in the medical center's planned program—and which would be an asset to any stroke rehabilitation program—is the showing of films that depict what has happened to a patient who has suffered a stroke, what can happen as a result, the type of nutrition needed, the type of outside help available, and so on. "The health field in general has become much more aware that a good education is a preventive measure and saves the patient and the family from stress as well," Aadahl says.

She predicts this preventive approach will catch on more strongly in the 1980s and beyond as the cost of medical care continues to escalate. She also predicts a growing demand for more education on preventive health care in local communities, particularly in day community centers for the elderly. Aadahl herself is active in such education programs, instructing the healthy in the warning signs of stroke and working with families after stroke has occurred.

In the latter case, she says, "one of the things we stress is that it is difficult to know the level of understanding of the patient, especially if he is aphasic. He may very well understand what's being said to him even though he can't communicate. So we encourage families to be careful what's said in front of him and never to use baby talk when trying to communicate." She emphasizes the importance of treating the stroke victim as an adult, carrying on a conversation in normal words and tones, and going to extra efforts, if necessary, to make sure the patient understands as much as possible.

"Nothing is as frustrating to a patient," she says, "as being treated like a child and knowing he is not in control."

CORRECTIVE THERAPY

Corrective therapy is, in effect, the next step after physical therapy in the physical rehabilitation process, but, as noted earlier, it is generally a therapy based in federal institutions such as a VA medical center. **In the ordinary community hospital, the work of the corrective therapist is generally incorporated in the program of physical therapy.**

While the physical therapist was re-educating Andy's muscles to function, the corrective therapist was putting those muscles to use. As Rehabilitation Coordinator Martin explains it, the corrective therapist puts the patient through strengthening exercises for the arms and legs, gait training, and walking. Once the physical therapist had Andy's leg muscles functioning, for example, the corrective therapist was concerned with teaching Andy to walk.

Though the corrective therapist may begin his work at the patient's bedside, usually his turn in the rehabilitation process comes after the patient's medical condition has stabilized and he is capable of being brought to the corrective therapy department. "We look at the patients' functional level," says Dennis W. Mullins, chief of corrective therapy at the Bay Pines VA Medical Center, "their ability to move their extremities, the functions they have retained, and their deficits in function. We also evaluate their cognition—their awareness—and the degree of cerebral involvement in the stroke, how much brain damage and what kinds of deficits they have."

These therapists test the patient's orientation to time, space, and his own person, determine whether he can follow directions, and determine the extent of his muscle movement in the affected parts of his body. Then the therapists decide on a type of program.

Some of the early evaluation tests include no more than having the patient squeeze the therapist's hand—as Dr. Romson tested Andy in the emergency room—push against his hand, resist the pushing pressure of the therapist's hand in return. These activities test the patient's extension and flexion, or bending, of the shoulders, elbows, and wrists. Knee straightening and flexing and similar ankle movements are lower extremity tests used at this stage.

During her exposure to the equipment in the various therapies, Amy was able to watch as therapists put Andy through some of his exercises. As he progressed, he was able to sit on an exercise table and raise and lower weights attached to his legs to test and improve his abilities at flexion and extension. Strength in his arms and shoulders was tested with the use of wall pulleys. His gait and walking ability were checked and improved through the use of parallel bars. Therapists tested whether he could achieve standing balance. They noted his breathing and pulse as he exercised, his endurance—how long he could walk using the parallel bars for support without getting too tired. As at Morton Plant Hospital, his ability to walk was also tested by having him walk without using the bars, with one or another form of assistance.

Although he followed a basic program, the program varies from patient to patient, depending on individual needs and abilities. Most of the time, Amy could not be there to watch him, since the therapists worked with him during the day. But on her days off, she took advantage of the opportunity offered by the physical therapist to observe his rehabilitation in action.

Like the physical therapist, the corrective therapist may also use biofeedback for muscle re-education. With advanced stroke-recovery patients who have regained some function but may suffer from hypertension, the corrective therapist may also employ a stress management program and progressive relaxation exercises. The aim, of course, is to lower the blood pressure by lowering the patient's anxiety level.

As Andy progressed, so did the therapists' aims—to teach him to make his transfers to and from the wheelchair independently, to make him independent when walking, first with the use of a walker, then a cane.

How much time a patient spends per session or per day in corrective therapy depends, as might be expected, on the patient. Rehabilitation coordinator Martin notes that patients usually are started with five to fifteen minutes on the overhead pulleys for exercising and stretching the shoulders, elbows, wrists, and hands. Then a similar time period may be devoted to testing and exercising their lower extremities, their legs attached to spring devices as they sit in their wheelchairs and straighten their knees, stretch their muscles, strengthen their legs. In between, Martin says, there is rest, rest, rest! Some patients, particularly in the early stages of recovery, tire easily. Others are probably undergoing physical and occupational therapy sessions the same day and may therefore be limited in the number of sessions they can tolerate. "If the patient is too tired," Mullins says, "the therapy won't work."

Mullins notes, too, that a corrective therapist might see a patient three times in a single day but work on different muscle groups on each visit. Today therapists use an isokinetic machine, once the patient has functional ability and can tolerate its pressure, that can measure his strength, range of motion, and endurance, calculate the results by computer, and provide them with a printout detailing the strengths and weaknesses of all the major muscles and joints of his body—hips, legs, knees, ankles, arms, shoulders, elbows, and wrists. It will tell the therapists not only what the problems are that they must deal with, but it will compare the strengths of the uninvolved limbs with those of the limbs affected by stroke.

Heavy exercise periods are limited to one a day. Andy's schedule might call for range-of-motion and strength exercises in the morning followed by rest at midday and then some walking exercise late in the day. The intensity of the program is based on what a patient can tolerate within his own limits. Here again Andy's age worked in his favor. Mullins finds that older patients are frequently more difficult to rehabilitate than younger ones. But Andy's weight worked against him. Of two patients who look essentially the same on evaluation, Mullins says, the heavier one, even if not grossly overweight, will be more difficult to rehabilitate. Patients whose weight is reasonably close to what it should be will usually make a faster return, achieve much more progress, and stabilize more quickly than obese patients.

Progress is sometimes measured in very small steps. It may be seen when a wheelchair patient is able to sit up straight, even though his right arm remains virtually useless. It could be seen in Andy when he was first able to stand up in the parallel bars without requiring assistance to get out of his wheelchair and when he could let go of the bars and stand straight. Such achievements can be very subtle or very dramatic.

As a rule of thumb, the therapists find that the major progress will occur within the first six to eight weeks, again pretty much in keeping with the "Rule of Three," discussed earlier. The therapists' goal in a rehabilitation unit is to get the patient home as soon as possible, but not to discharge him before he is ready for home care, either by a home therapist or by his spouse or family.

Part of that discharge decision is based on an evaluation of the person who will be taking care of him at home. Here again the therapist works with the whole stroke team in discharge planning, helping to determine what kind of adaptation will be needed by the patient and family, integrating where possible the family members into the therapy area so that they learn the necessary skills that will help them in handling the patient after he returns home.

If the patient has a very capable spouse, he may be sent home far earlier than the patient whose spouse will have difficulty in caring for him. If, as in Amy's case, there will be no one home to care for him, then the patient must achieve a greater degree of independence before he can be discharged.

Ideally, the therapists do a home evaluation, talking with the spouse, setting up an exercise program for the patient to follow at home, even visiting the discharged patient at home as often as necessary while teaching the caregiver to work with the patient. The therapist may also determine if any special equipment is needed in the home. The Veterans Administration system will provide medically prescribed equipment such as a seat for the tub or a rail for a wall beside the toilet without charge, subject to certain cost limitations and eligibility requirements. A medical center may also have a home-care team to evaluate the home for its accessibility, to suggest adaptive equipment, and to assist the patient while the spouse learns to provide the care. The team usually includes a physician, nurse, social worker, rehabilitation therapist, and dietitian. We will look at home care at the community level in more detail later.

As a spouse or other caregiver develops confidence, the therapists gradually step aside and let him or her take over. "If the patient is motivated and has a confident caregiver," Mullins says, "he'll get more intense and frequent therapy at home than he would in a hospital. The monitoring therapist will keep upgrading the program until the patient reaches his potential."

OCCUPATIONAL THERAPY

Occupational therapy teaches patients self-care skills they have lost due to the effects of stroke. Andy's relearning began in Morton Plant Hospital with basic hygiene and feeding and extended through his therapy to dressing and performing other activities of daily living, everything he needed to know to acclimate to his environment. This retraining is also tailored to the patient's sex and often to his or her previous lifestyle and interests.

Like the other therapists, the occupational therapist starts off with an evaluation of the patient, generally after he has stabilized and been brought to the OT clinic. Through fairly intensive testing, his alertness, his reflexes, muscle tone, strength, motor coordination, dexterity, range of motion, sensation, and perception of things around him are measured, as are his ability to swallow and other oral functions.

The therapist is particularly interested in his perception, since patients with impaired body image may ignore or neglect their involved side, and that will extend to the activities of daily living, such as bathing and grooming. Of course, the therapist must also know how well the patient can communicate, can understand, can remember instructions, solve problems, and follow directions. In addition, since the patient has lost all or some use of one side of his body, the therapist wants to know whether other conditions, such as arthritis in the side unaffected by stroke, will hinder the therapist's efforts and the patient's ability to substitute the use of his unaffected hand and arm for the hand and arm disabled by stroke.

The goal of the occupational therapist is much the same as that of other stroke therapists. As expressed by Donna Archer, chief of the Occupational Therapy Section at the Bay Pines VA facility, **it is to have the patient** functioning as independently as possible and to get the involved parts of his body to their highest functional level.

Many times, Archer explains, that means the occupational therapist must work on the patient's body awareness as well as on muscle re-education before proceeding to teach the patient a specific activity.

On one of her weekdays off, Amy also had the chance to go through the occupational therapy facilities and to watch Andy at work, learning dexterity with his left hand by knitting with the aid of an assistive device. It was only one of the many new skills he was learning, which started with the basic ones of eating, washing, brushing his teeth, and other aspects of personal grooming. Since Andy is a right hemiplegic, he had to learn to put on his shoes, button a jacket or shirt, and perform other customary functions with his left hand, a totally new experience for him and for most other patients in his situation. At later stages, the activities to be taught became more advanced. The model kitchen Amy was shown through could provide invaluable help for the days when Andy would be required to take care of himself at home.

Just as the occupational therapist must prod overcautious right hemiplegics like Andy to progress, so she must slow down the impulsive left hemiplegics who may try to race through every process, skipping steps as they go. Obviously, that means the occupational therapist must develop a specific plan for each individual patient. The therapist may see a patient once, twice, or more times a day, depending on his need and progress, with each session lasting about half an hour.

For some patients, the technique of putting on a shirt or blouse with one hand can be learned in one session. For others, the patient with perceptual problems for example, just recognizing that he or she must put each arm into a sleeve of a garment may take a great deal of time and effort and require repeated instructions.

Often the occupational therapist will put the patient's affected arm in a "support system" or sling to help realign the shoulder joint. She may also put a splint on his affected hand to help maintain it in a functional position.

Archer notes that the focus of occupational therapy has shifted in recent years from less therapeutic arts and crafts to more exercise routine. Nevertheless, if you were to look in on an occupational therapist at work with a stroke patient, you might see a phase of rehabilitation that seems like fun. One of Andy's exercises was to catch a basketball bounced on the floor in front of him. Amy would have enjoyed it more if Andy had been more adept, but it pained her to see him struggling for balance and coordination, both of which he gained as his therapy progressed. In another exercise, a therapist and patient might toss a bean bag back and forth or engage in what looked like a card game. Actually, the bean bag exercise is aimed at giving the patient practice in his finger-release mechanism, and the card game is an exercise in teaching the patient sequence—putting the cards in order, two, three, four, and so on.

"Many aspects of occupational therapy are activity oriented," Archer says, "to make them more interesting to the patient and in that way to improve his or her motivation."

Much as a child develops from birth, so a patient recovering from stroke must go through specific developmental patterns and reflexes in order to achieve normal movement. The occupational therapist uses various special techniques to assist the patient to progress through these stages. Nor is the patient always aware of his own progress on a day-to-day basis. Andy today remembers the exercises well, but he was unaware at the time of how they were helping him.

Occupational therapy also makes use of a number of "assistive devices" to help the patient adapt to his disability—ranging from button-hook type gadgets to help him in dressing to a device that blocks food from slipping off a patient's plate as he struggles to eat with one hand to a knife for cutting meat that can be used with one hand; rather than slice the meat, the patient uses the knife in a rocking motion to sever a piece of meat. Andy used many of the devices during the course of his therapy but eventually progressed to the point where the "rocker" knife was the only assistance he needed. Any time he did not have one available, Amy was there to cut his meat for him. His progress mirrors the motive behind the devices: to help the patient reach the goal of functional independence.

The outcome of a patient's efforts is dependent on many factors. A primary one, as noted previously, is motivation, something Andy had in abundance because of his supportive family. But motivation also depends in part on the type of stroke the patient suffered, the extent of its damage, and the environment. There is always the battle with depression to be fought.

Patients may also be affected by their previous exposure to stroke, Archer says. If they've seen a relative or friend make a good recovery from stroke, they have a better idea of what they can accomplish. But if their experience has been with a stroke victim who is severely impaired, they may expect that outcome for themselves. Andy's exposure had been to two female relatives, but because both of them were elderly when their strokes occurred, he did not relate to their infirmities. Instead, his comparative youthfulness coupled with Amy's optimism led him to echo Amy's expectations of recovery.

Patient personalities are also a factor. Some people are naturally fearful while others have a tendency to plow ahead regardless of the problems to be overcome. Andy was naturally outgoing and aggressive before his stroke, and those attitudes were reflected in how he performed in therapy—although they were modified somewhat by the effect of his right hemiplegia and by the loss of emotional control, especially in the early stages of his recovery, due to the effects of stroke itself.

"Family support makes a great deal of difference," Archer says. "If two patients have the same side affected with the same degree of severity, the patient with family support will probably do better in recovering because he'll be anxious to get out of the hospital and get home." Home was certainly where Andy Robertson wanted to go.

As with the other therapies, the ideal occupational therapy program includes the patient's spouse, especially if he is going directly home rather than to a nursing home. The therapist designs a treatment plan for the family to follow and puts the patient through it with the spouse or other supportive family members present so they can observe what the patient can do and needs to learn to do.

"Some wives like to help a lot," Archer says, "and they may help more than they should. We try to teach them to let the stroke patient take a bit longer, if necessary, in getting dressed, for instance, because it's better for him if he can dress independently."

Because the VA Medical Center at Bay Pines has associated with some forty nursing homes in its surrounding area, it tries to place patients who need further assistance in homes near their own homes. Community hospitals may also follow this course in their immediate areas, though the number of homes available may be far fewer. Again, the feeling is that if a patient is in a nursing home where his family visits him frequently, that might often be a motivating factor for him to regain ability or at least make him more receptive to a further rehabilitation program.

In addition, both the hospitals and the VA medical centers offer outpatient rehabilitation care and can arrange home care for patients who no longer need institutional care.

T·H·I·R·T·E·E·N
POST-HOSPITAL CARE

Extended care may be for a short duration or it may be a prelude to long-term home care.

INSTITUTIONAL/HOME REHABILITATION

HOME EXERCISES

A ndy's long stay at the VA Medical Center encompassed many types of care that could otherwise have been provided in a variety of institutions. Ordinarily, a social services worker will advise the family of a stroke patient of the resources available in his community when the period of acute hospital care comes to an end. Relatively few communities have formal rehabilitation institutions, but many have some form of home health services. The choice of the post-hospital care will depend on the availability of facilities and services, their location, the patient's needs, the cost to the patient, and his or her insurance coverage.

A rehabilitation hospital or a rehabilitation unit within a hospital, such as the one in which Andy was treated at the VA Medical Center, provides the most extensive care. It offers basic patient care as well as the support and therapeutic services and usually discharges a patient after about three to four weeks of treatment. Ideally, a rehabilitation facility should be within easy visiting distance from home for the patient's spouse and family, so that family members also can provide support and can learn their own responsibilities for the day when the patient will be coming home to stay.

Skilled nursing facilities or extended-care units, which Andy experienced at a later stage of his stay at the Medical Center, offer a second line of care for patients who need continuous nursing care, limited rehabilitation, and some assistance in their own self-care. Although Andy continued his recovery under such care, these facilities typically serve patients who probably won't substantially improve with intensive rehabilitation. Extended care may be for a short duration or, for patients in whom little progress in functional recovery can be expected, it may be a prelude to long-term home care.

Intermediate care facilities may serve a patient who needs only minimal medical or nursing care but must be given attention in the protective environment of a health-care institution.

State or county institutions for the chronically ill are another resource. Still others include domiciliary or resident-care facilities. These "foster homes," which are sometimes available through fraternal organizations or charitable or government agencies, aim to provide a homelike environment, with some supervision in personal care along with board and shelter.

The goal in Andy's treatment, however, as in, the treatment of most stroke patients, was to send the patient home eventually. In 1969, Medicare certified almost 2,500 agencies to provide home health care as a Medicare-covered benefit. The number has fluctuated since that time, but, in general, the pressure today for shortened hospital stays is likely to improve the numbers and availability of such agencies.

What kinds of care do they provide? Of the original 2,400 to 2,500 agencies, 100 percent provided nursing care in the home, about 75 percent offered physical therapy, more than 25 percent provided speech therapists, and more than 20 percent had occupational therapists and social services assistance.

Essentially, qualified home health agencies are simply independent businesses that sell their services in the community. They are licensed by their states along with being certified by the federal Medicare program. To them falls the job of providing part-time skilled health care as well as training the spouse or other family member to take over the role of caregiver.

As with other stroke rehabilitation services, the patient must be referred to home health care by his family doctor, who stipulates which services the patient is to receive. In addition to providing nursing care and the various therapies, a home health agency may also offer light housekeeping services and, through its social worker, may be able to refer the family to other sources of help within the community.

Ideally, the stroke team at the community hospital or, in its absence, the family doctor, has already evaluated the patient and determined which home health services he will need. The family will be expected to take an active role in providing them. One of the first steps the stroke care *Guidelines* suggest for the family is professional counseling. Just as the patient may need counseling to help him cope with his anxieties, fears, and hostilities, so the family may need counseling to ease its adjustment to the new situation.

In addition, the *Guidelines* list fourteen services that the homebound patient might require, such as the services of a physician and the various nurses, therapists, and counselors, evaluation of the physical aspects of the home and recommendations for changes, householder assistance, financial help, a friendly visitor service, and sometimes vocational assistance and the provision of meals.

If a spouse is to serve at home without home health agency assistance, the *Guidelines* point out, she or he should receive counseling on the changes in roles within the family that result from the stroke and the new family ground rules. From the doctor or hospital therapists, a spouse should have a schedule of home treatment outlined to her or him where appropriate. The spouse may also have to reorganize the home environment to accommodate the patient's disabilities and have to make social contacts for the patient to stimulate his interest in the activities of everyday life and in work or hobbies.

Such formal home health care was not in the plan for Andy. The goal of his extensive rehabilitation therapy was to bring him to the point where he could function independently at home once he was discharged. If Amy considered discharge at all at this stage, it was only with fear. Despite Andy's progress, she did not feel he was mentally alert enough yet to cope with being alone all day in the house. Her employment would also prevent her from assisting him in the functions and exercises he would have to perform at home.

For spouses whose stroke victims do come home early in the recovery period, a series of simple exercises, with the guidance and approval of the family doctor and therapists, can help tone the patient's muscles and keep his joints from becoming stiff. Following are exercises adapted with permission from the U.S. Public Health Service's illustrated booklet *Strike Back at Stroke*, which is distributed by the American Heart Association and its affiliates. As the booklet cautions, no exercise should be done unless it is prescribed or approved by the doctor directly or through his representative health therapist.

It is important to remember, too, that the limbs on *both* sides of the patient's body should be exercised the same number of times to prevent the unaffected muscles from becoming weak.

HOME EXERCISES

These exercises are designed for the caregiver to provide while the patient is in bed.

ARMS

Exercise 1

1. With the patient lying on his back in bed, extend his arm straight down alongside his body, the palm of his hand to the mattress.

2. Place one of your hands above the patient's elbow and hold his hand with your other hand.

3. Raise the arm straight up, slowly and gently, bringing it perpendicular to the bed and then continuing straight back as far as it will go until it is resting on the bed alongside his head. The arm may be bent at the elbow if the headboard prevents you from extending it full length straight back past his head.

4. Bring the arm back in the same motion to the starting position and repeat the exercise the number of times prescribed. Then follow the same process with the other arm.

Exercise 2

1. As with Exercise 1, with the patient's arm extended straight down alongside his body in bed, palm down, place one of your hands above his elbow and take his hand in your other hand.

2. Move the arm toward you and away from his body, slowly bringing it around toward his head, as far as it will go without hurting him. Bending the arm at the elbow will enable you to extend it over the top of his head and avoid the headboard.

3. Return the arm by the same circular motion to the starting position.

Exercise 3

1. Extend the patient's arm straight out from his body, palm up.

2. Place one hand on the arm above the elbow and hold the patient's hand with your other hand.

3. Lift the arm up and bring it across the patient's chest.

4. Return the arm to the starting position.

Exercise 4

1. Extend the patient's upper arm away from his body, bend it at the elbow, and extend his lower arm downward on the bed parallel to the body.

2. Hold the upper arm against the mattress.

3. Take the patient's hand with your other hand and raise it, bringing his lower arm upright perpendicular to the bed and continuing the movement back as far as you can go toward his head without hurting him. Hold the upper arm in place against the mattress.

4. With the lower arm resting alongside the head, reverse the process and return the lower arm to the starting position.

Exercise 5

1. As in the preceding exercise, the patient's upper arm is extended away from his body, his elbow is bent, but this time take his hand and raise the lower arm perpendicular to the bed.

2. Gently twist the palm of the hand toward the patient's face.

3. Twist the hand back in the opposite direction.

Exercise 6

1. With the patient's lower arm perpendicular to the bed as in Exercise 5, hold the patient's wrist with one hand.

2. With your other hand, keep the fingers of the patient's hand straight and bend the hand backward.

3. Straighten the hand.

4. Bend the hand forward, closing the fingers to make a fist.

5. Open the hand.

Exercise 7

1. With the patient's lower arm upraised as before, hold his fingers straight with one of your hands.

2. With your other hand, bend the patient's thumb into the palm of his hand.

3. Pull the thumb back so that it points away from the hand and repeat the exercise.

4. Move the thumb in a circle.

LEGS

Exercise 1

1. With the patient's legs extended straight down the bed and the patient lying on his back, place one of your hands under his knee and the other on the back of the heel of his foot.

2. Lift his leg off the bed and bend it at the knee.

3. With the knee bent, push the leg straight back slowly toward the patient's head as far as it will go without hurting him.

4. Straighten the knee by raising the foot upward.

5. Lower the leg to the starting position.

Exercise 2

1. With the patient's legs fully extended on the bed, again place one hand under his knee and put the other on the heel of the foot.

2. Lift the leg straight up and bend it to a right angle at the knee.

3. Hold the knee in place and gently pull the foot sideways toward you.

4. Move the foot back to the starting position.

5. Now push the foot away from you toward the opposite side of the bed.

6. Move the foot back to the starting position.

Exercise 3

1. With the patient's legs fully extended, place one hand under his knee and the other under his heel.

2. Holding the leg straight, lift it about 2 inches off the mattress.

3. Pull the leg toward you.

4. Push the leg back to the starting position.

Exercise 4

1. With the patient's heel against the mattress, place your hand under it so that your arm presses against the bottom of the patient's foot lengthwise from toe to heel.

2. Place your other hand around the patient's ankle from the front.

3. Press your arm against the bottom of the foot, pushing the foot backward toward the leg. At the same time, pull on the heel of the foot as though you were trying to stretch the leg.

4. Move your arm back to the starting position.

5. With that hand still gripping the heel in the starting position, slide your other hand along to grip the foot just below the toes.

6. Push down on the foot with that hand to "point" the toes. At the same time, push up against the heel with the other hand.

7. Return to the starting position.

Exercise 5

1. With the leg extended straight downward, the back of the heel flat on the mattress, put one hand around the ankle from the front, and with the other hand grip the ball of the foot just below the toes.

2. Turn the whole foot outward.

3. Turn the whole foot inward.

Exercise 6

1. Gripping the instep of the foot with one hand, place the other against the bottom of the toes.

2. Push back on the toes toward the leg.

3. Push down on the toes.

Similar versions of many of these exercises can be used by the patient himself as he progresses through his recovery. Again, they should be performed with the guidance of an appropriate health-care professional.

Another U.S. Public Health Service booklet, *Up and Around*, also distributed by the American Heart Association, provides an illustrated guide to the patient in performing such functions as rolling over in bed, getting up and sitting on the side of the bed, moving from a sitting position on the edge of the bed to a lying position, wheelchair transfers, dressing, walking with an assistive device such as a cane, climbing stairs, and stepping up or down curbs.

Therapists have devised many other exercises and techniques that patients can perform on their own or with assistance at home to enhance their rehabilitation as their recovery period progresses. The following are suggested by Rafael H. Vega, chief physical therapist at the Fort Bayard, New Mexico, Medical Center, as evolving from the work of many in the field to improve the patient's balance and his ability to bear his weight on his affected limbs. The patient should be safeguarded in performing these exercises and will probably need assistance at first. Vega also recommends that the exercises be performed on a firm mat, where appropriate, and in front of a mirror to stimulate progress.

Prone position
The patient lies on his stomach and puts his weight on his elbows and forearms. When he has achieved satisfactory balance in that position, he raises his unaffected arm, extending it in front of him and bearing his weight on his affected elbow and forearm.

To practice extension of the elbows, the prone patient assumes the push-up position, keeping both hands flat on the surface below him.

Kneeling
For balance, the patient kneels erectly on both knees. Later he kneels on alternate knees.

Sitting
The patient is placed in a sitting position with his back unsupported. He places the hand of his affected arm on the knee of his affected leg or a firm surface and pushes downward while leaning toward the affected side and extending his elbow as fully as he can. Assistance will probably be needed at first in this as in other exercises. This technique will help him control the tendency of stroke patients to fall toward the affected side.

When he can maintain his sitting balance adequately in this way, the caregiver can tap the patient's shoulder toward the affected side, thereby forcing him to resist physical pressure pushing him toward his weak side and improve his balance control.

To practice weight-bearing in the sitting position, the patient sits with his legs extended in front of him and puts a hand flat on the floor on each side behind him. Then he props himself up on his hands, rolling his shoulders outward. A pillow under his thighs helps provide greater transfer of weight to the shoulders.

Standing
The patient takes one step forward and then one step backward on the unaffected leg while he shifts his weight to the affected leg. This movement will help him to develop a weight-shifting technique for use of the unaffected leg when walking.

To practice hip and knee extension, the patient stands before a 3- or 4-inch-high step, places the foot of his affected leg on the step, and steps up with that foot. He may require hand support at first.

The patient can also practice weight-bearing by pushing against resistance with the heel of his hand, extending his elbow as fully as possible. He might practice that technique by pushing against the frame of a door, using the unaffected arm to assist him, if necessary, in gaining elbow extension.

Turning the head toward the side involved in the stroke and tapping the shoulder to increase pressure in balance exercises is also recommended.

Again, none of these exercises should be undertaken without approval of the health professional involved in the patient's care, and precautions should be taken for the patient's safety.

F·O·U·R·T·E·E·N

THE
ROAD TO
RECOVERY

*I didn't expect anything of him,
so everything he did
was just like a miracle.*

AMY ROBERTSON

B right posters, mirrors, and various pieces of rehabilitation equipment such as overhead pulleys and special skills-training devices adorn the walls and poke out from the cabinets in the various therapy departments where the VA rehabilitates its patients. About half the patients who go through the rehab units are stroke victims; the others include amputees and patients with a wide range of problems.

Andy was put through his paces. Still relying heavily on a wheelchair, he worked on the parallel bars to improve his walking ability and endurance, progressing to a walker and eventually to a cane. Meanwhile, in occupational therapy, he continued to learn how to clothe himself, shave with his left hand, comb his hair. He found brushing and washing his hair with just the use of his left arm one of the most difficult problems to deal with. He participated in exercises while in his wheelchair and, by the end of March, he was back at speech therapy in earnest, trying to bring forth new words to replace the "you" he said in answer to almost everything during the earlier stage of his recovery. A foot/ankle brace gave added strength to his damaged leg, and elastic stockings reduced the swelling in his lower legs. Because the leg is not supplied by the same middle cerebral artery, neurologist Jackson explains, a stroke resulting from damage to that artery, as in Andy's case, spares the leg somewhat relative to the arm. Since most strokes are middle cerebral artery strokes, Jackson says, the leg will recover more often and generally to a better degree than the arm. An anterior cerebral artery stroke, on the other hand, would affect the leg more.

Andy's ability to use his damaged leg improved appreciably as his stay at the VA Medical Center lengthened. Biofeedback became part of his life for muscle re-education, and the passive range of motion of his arms and legs remained normal, a good sign with regard to his muscles and joints. His gait was mildly off balance, but he was improving in the parallel bars, moving up and down the bars several times at a session without assistance, the therapist barely keeping a hand on him in case he started to fall. Training in walking outside the parallel bars soon progressed. Still, Andy clung to his dependence on his wheelchair as a child might hold on to a security blanket.

His overall anxiety was a problem his caregivers and family had to deal with. Not only can this be a feature of right hemiplegia, but it is almost to be expected when a person, especially an outgoing, communicative person like Andy Robertson, becomes shut off by a wall of silence he has difficulty breaking through. His progress in speech therapy was slow, although it was also becoming evident. "Yes" and "no," used appropriately, replaced the "you," and other words began to force their way out.

Nevertheless, both the damage caused by the stroke and the lasting effects of the stroke had, especially in Amy's view, altered Andy's personality. "Essentially," Amy says, "the big change in Andy was impatience, and that was brought on by his frustration over not being able to talk and do the things he formerly could do. I can't blame him, but he became terribly impatient."

She frequently let Andy know when he was exhibiting problem behavior, but he seemed unable to alter it. "Do you recognize that you're being impatient with me or with the children?" Amy would ask him. "Yes," Andy would reply in a calmer moment. "Isn't there anything you can do about it?" "No." "It just comes on," Amy says, "and it gets extreme." It was a door-slamming type of impatience that disturbed the family.

One thing that had not changed was Andy's approach to his appearance. Always well-groomed before, as his awareness grew, he began to strive for a neat appearance again, even though he spent most of his time in pajamas. That attitude helped him develop some of the motivation he needed to keep progressing in the various therapies as well. Fortunately for his progress, motivation was a quality continuously supplied by Amy and his family, especially at those times when apathy and depression seemed to be taking over.

"Motivation is vital to anybody who has ever had a stroke of any type at any age," his family physician, Dr. Romson, says. "Some patients won't continue therapy long enough, speech therapy, for instance. They get so frustrated and so aggravated at not being able to speak that they don't even want to try."

The same is true for recovering some strength in the disabled arm or leg, he adds, particularly if the limbs are completely paralyzed as Andy's were in the beginning. "That's where the therapists can help so much," he says, "can encourage the patient. The younger the patient is and the more willing he is to get things done, the easier it is to motivate him. This man was motivated. He wanted to recover, and he worked at it."

A milestone in that motivation and rehabilitation process occurred in June. On June 30, Andy would be forty-eight years old. What better birthday present for the whole Robertson family, Amy thought, than for Andy to celebrate that birthday at home?

Amy's sister and brother-in-law came to Florida that June to visit her parents, and the family planned a homecoming dinner for Andy's birthday. Amy got special permission from the Medical Center for him to go home for the night; the institution even supplied a wheelchair for the occasion.

As a surprise to his mother and the family, Doug built a ramp so the wheelchair could be moved into and out of the house more easily. He kept it hidden until Amy and her visiting relatives left for the hospital and then put it in place against the front step.

Andy waited anxiously for them at the hospital. "We had all his clothes with us," Amy says, "but as he started to dress, he knew something was missing. We couldn't understand what he was trying to tell us, but we knew he wanted something. For many minutes we went through charades to try to figure out what it was. Then we hurried him along because we knew the whole family was waiting. Finally, he was dressed, and he got through to us: We had forgotten his belt."

That first visit home was the biggest thrill the family had in Andy's whole recovery process. "Everyone rushed out to meet the car when we arrived," Amy says. "We were so green we needed a lot of help in getting him out. We didn't know what to do or how to do it."

The ramp came as a pleasant surprise and the family pushed Andy in his chair up the incline and into the house. His mother, the children, and Amy's family all fussed over him. Duke, the gray poodle, hadn't seen Andy since the night of the stroke. "The dog went absolutely crazy over him," Amy says. "It was such a great accomplishment—to have him home."

Amy cooked outside on a grill, a sort of picnic-style dinner of hamburgers and hot dogs that she knew Andy would enjoy. Every passing minute someone doted on him—did he need anything to drink, to eat, did he want to go to the bathroom. "He was so fragile," Amy says. "We treated him like he couldn't even think for himself. We did everything for him, and we worried so about him. We wouldn't let him do anything."

Andy did manage to manipulate his wheelchair about, but he had trouble getting through the doorways and was consantly bumping into something, leaving marks on the walls and woodwork some of which still attest to his first homecoming.

The large birthday cake had only five candles on it to make it easier for Andy to blow them out. He did—one at a time, and the family joined in choruses of "Happy Birthday." "It was a milestone," Amy says. "I probably couldn't have done it if the family hadn't been here and given me their support. It was very hard to take Andy back to Bay Pines when the time came."

It was hard, too, for Andy. Once the family got him settled in the car again, Sally accompanied Amy on the trip back to the Medical Center. Andy cried.

The birthday celebration was the first of many short visits home. Meanwhile, by July, Andy's stay in the rehabilitation unit far exceeded the normal length of stay there, which Dr. Smith, Chief of the Rehabilitation Medicine Service at the Medical Center, puts at twenty-one days on average today. Chiefly it was Amy's fearful reluctance to take him home permanently to an empty house that kept him there. But the stroke team had now reached the point where the members agreed it was time for Andy to leave the rehabilitation unit. They also came up with an alternative, and it gave Amy a shock: Andy was to be transferred to the nursing home on the grounds of the Medical Center.

"When they called me and said they were transferring him to the nursing home, I almost had a heart attack," Amy says. "I pictured it as a regular nursing home, and I thought they had given up on him. 'That's it,' I told myself. 'They're just going to leave him there to wilt away.'"

Amy fought the move. She phoned various representatives at the Medical Center and tried to convince them to keep Andy in the rehabilitation unit. She told them Andy would be disappointed if his surroundings were changed. She said he wouldn't do well in new surroundings. She argued that he would just give up. Her whole campaign was another milestone, this time in Amy's behavior. She lost the battle, but she grew in confidence from waging it.

"As it turned out," she says, "they knew what they were doing. They transferred him, and they continued his therapy."

A report from the Medical Center's Social Services Department on July 14 details the situation. The report notes that Andy was now receiving a monthly VA pension of $261 and that his application for Social Security disability benefits had been turned down because he had not paid enough into the program. Amy's salary was put at $5,500 a year, and note was made of the mortgage on their house. Said the report:

"Veteran is alert, responsive individual who has shown good motivation in the rehabilitation process. He appears accepting of a need for continued care in a protective environment to both insure his present level of functioning and to provide him with maximum opportunity for improvement.

"Mrs. Robertson, after some initial anxiety regarding the aspect of a change for her husband, is now most accepting of the [nursing home] referral. She takes him home frequently on weekend passes and does indicate that he seems to experience some depression some of these times. She feels, and correctly so, that the home environment more forcibly points out to her husband the changes and limitations brought about by his illness. The children have been and are extremely supportive and understanding of their parents' problems.

"A return home at this time would be detrimental, as it is necessary that Mrs. Robertson continue with her employment, and she would not be able to provide him with needed care and therapy. As previously noted, he is alert, cooperative, and highly motivated. It would seem he would have a favorable prognosis for continuing improvement opportunities offered by the [nursing home] as well as being able to progress with his speech therapy."

At that time, the nursing home consisted of one building, completed in 1971, housing 120 beds in two-bed and four-bed rooms. A second building was added in 1981, and together the two are regarded as the posh hotel of the Medical Center, "the kind of hotel you might go to on vacation," Amy says. Beautiful, wide windows in the dayroom face out on Boca Ciega Bay and on the wooden pier jutting into it. The Sunshine Skyway over Tampa Bay in the distance offers a magnificent view, and Madeira Beach, across the water from the home and where patients are sometimes taken for outings, shows a promise of what might lie ahead for the rehabilitated patient. Bright, airy patient rooms look out on courtyards where patients and visitors may sit on benches under shady trees and plan for the future, the windows of the rooms designed to make the most of the winter or summer sun.

Contrary to Amy's initial expectations, some of the patients in the nursing home were not patients who simply needed custodial care. They were patients who had potential for further rehabilitation. Recreational therapy and group exercises, including sessions for those dependent on wheelchairs, were added to Andy's program—but Andy took them standing up.

"One of the first things they did at the nursing home was to take his wheelchair away," Amy says. "I thought it was cruel. It was like the end of the world for him. I asked myself what he was going to do now that he no longer had the wheelchair to get around in. The answer was that he started walking and then getting stronger!"

Early reports in Andy's medical record at the nursing home indicate his status at that time:

August 1: "It is my impression that his comprehension is fairly intact. He's unable to articulate his needs due to aphasia, but he does respond on a 'yes' or 'no' level and he indicates by head-shaking when the interviewer misinterprets his responses. He is alert, cooperative, friendly, and well motivated to improve his present status."

August 2: "Appears a little frightened and apprehensive, as does wife. Both need emotional support and practical reassurance. Time will help as he recovers use of body and speech."

August 15: A physical therapist notes: "He is capable of independent ambulation with a crutch. Transfers well. Range of motion is within normal limits. Needs increased activity tolerance and maintenance of range of motion."

About this time, a list of fifty questions was put to Andy to explore more deeply his attitude and prospects. Perhaps the most significant answer was to the question "Who is the person most important to you?" His answer was his wife.

Andy made a special friend at the nursing home, another stroke victim named Ed Moore. Most of the residents of the home were older, but Ed was about Andy's age and had a young family. He was also a right hemiplegic and was unable to speak. They weren't roommates at first, but, given their growing association and patient transfers and discharges, they were soon sharing a two-bed room.

Amy enjoyed watching their friendship grow. "They would just sit in silence, but they felt close to each other," she says. "Ed's wife and I would visit with them. She'd tell me how Ed was coming along, and I'd tell her about Andy, and they'd share in the conversation just by listening."

Ed's example also inspired Andy. "I used to be envious of his wife at first because Ed was so sturdy when he'd do physical therapy," Amy says. "The therapist would take the basketball and bounce it on the floor hard in front of him, and he'd catch it without tottering. Then the therapist would do that to Andy, and Andy would almost fall over. So I was envious. I thought, 'Oh, if only Andy could be sturdy like that.'"

Andy had already learned to feed himself, and now his therapists made him rely more on himself for other things. "As soon as Andy got over there," Amy says, "we brought his clothes to him. He had to dress completely every day. That was part of the rehabilitation."

Andy also showered and shaved himself daily—though he often waited for Amy to arrive in the evening to assist him. He brushed his teeth, combed his hair, and in general put into operation all the things he'd been taught to do by the therapists since he began his recovery from stroke—and all using only his left hand. He wore short-sleeve, button shirts—never a pullover, which is far more difficult for stroke patients with a disabled arm to deal with—and he buttoned them with his left hand. He wore no special clothing, though such is available for stroke patients. His fastidiousness had not changed; Andy was still a very neat dresser.

"Every step he took at Bay Pines was a high spot," Amy says. "I didn't expect anything of him by this time, so everything he did was just like a miracle, even if it was small. It was at the nursing home that he learned to be more confident. That's where Andy finally got on his own."

What gave both of them the most satisfaction was Andy's progress in walking. "That was the most important thing," Amy says, "and then he was independent. He could take me around the home and show me where the various therapies were given." Through those little walks from unit to unit, Amy also was participating in his rehabilitation, encouraging his ambulation and giving him reason to develop his walking ability further.

One evening, when she arrived after work as usual, Andy had a surprise for her. He suggested they go "out" for a walk. That was the first time they'd been able to set off independently together for a walk on the grounds. They walked to the Medical Center's administration building several buildings away. Soon they were repeating that walk frequently as Andy's strength and confidence grew. "It was not only physical therapy," Amy says, "it motivated him because it got him to see the outside world instead of just sitting in the home all the time."

Amy had taken another step, too, to get Andy back into the "outside world." Their walking excursions were not their first ventures onto the hospital grounds. As Andy's interest in life around him continued to grow, he wanted to be more familiar with his surroundings. So he and Amy began a nightly drive. Every night during her visit, they'd leave the building with permission and drive around the perimeter of the Medical Center grounds.

"He wanted to get out," Amy says, "and I think it did him good to get into the car and go for a little ride and see something different."

Meanwhile, as indicated in the Social Services Department report, there were more visits home. By September, Andy was spending every weekend there with his family. "I'd pick him up after I finished work on Fridays, and I'd have him back by 7:00 p.m. on Sundays. They let us bring the wheelchair home, and he'd go around the house by himself in it, still banging up doors and woodwork."

Even though Andy showed some periods of depression at home, he was generally happy to be there—until Sunday nights. Then Amy, usually with Sally's help, would drive him back to the nursing home. He always cried.

Time at the nursing home, however, was growing short for Andy Robertson. The chief factor keeping him there at this point—as it had been all along—was Amy's unwillingness to take him home because of her inability to be there to care for him. It was a formidable reason, but one that now had to be confronted. An evaluation of Andy was done in November, and a date of December 18 was set as the deadline for his discharge.

An entry in his record on November 16 indicates that Amy was surprised when a therapist told her that Andy planned to be home by that December date. The record also indicates that she was concerned. "Resident and wife need assistance in resolving conflict regarding discharge," the record entry states. "Wife feels overwhelmed about meeting the resident's needs, fears for his safety."

Indeed, those fears were very strong in Amy. What she needed, she decided, was an ally to help her fight this latest proposed change in Andy's life and her own. She telephoned Andy's speech therapist at the VA Medical Center, with whom she had built a warm rapport over the months of Andy's rehabilitation. "I was looking for support," Amy says. "I told her I didn't think he was well enough to come home. Actually, I didn't think he could do anything. I didn't have any confidence in him then, and we were so worried about leaving him alone."

She didn't get the sympathy and support she'd hoped for. Instead, she got a lecture aimed at giving her the confidence she needed. "She told me that leaving him at the nursing home was a cop-out. I thought it over, and I felt she was right."

The stroke team scheduled a meeting, and Amy, her mother-in-law, Eleanor, and her daughter Sally attended. It was in the nursing home, and Amy found her small party greatly outnumbered by the therapists, doctors, chaplain, everyone Andy had been in contact with during his therapy there. Andy was also present. "They had all evaluated him," Amy says, "and they all felt he was ready to come home." With fears still unresolved, Amy acquiesced. A brief account of that meeting was entered in Andy's medical record essentially as follows:

— 131 —

December 5: "Wife was reluctant to care for the veteran at home. She stated her hesitation about his abilities to care for himself if he was going to be home alone. He stated firmly his desire to be discharged on December 16. Wife agreed with veteran's request when it was determined that the maximum benefit had been achieved. She verbally agreed and appeared accepting. The resident agreed to be more assertive in the house and to take a greater part in the decision-making."

It was her talk with the speech therapist that had made the difference, Amy says. Without that counseling, she would have fought the change.

On December 16, 1977, after 319 total days of hospitalization, Andy Robertson, his wife at his side, made his departure from the Veterans Administration Medical Center at Bay Pines, Florida, and went home. Their excitement can only be imagined. Yet they were filled with a sadness, too. Ed Moore and the other men with whom Andy had shared his months in the nursing home would be staying. They shared painful good-bys, the more painful because Amy and Andy knew that most of the men there were too disabled ever to go home. The good-by to Ed Moore would have been still more painful if they had known then that they would never see him again. His turn for discharge was to come less than two weeks later, and he would be moved a thousand miles away. They lost track of him. Andy cried and laughed alternately as he tried to overcome with humor the sorrow of departure. They drove off, knowing that a dramatic change was occurring in their lives. It was too soon to realize what that would mean.

Two weeks later, when they returned to the medical center for Andy's first checkup as an outpatient, their approach to that change came into clearer focus. Here, in part, is the note that appears in his record:

December 29: "Resident communicates his great pleasure at discharge and feels that his leaving proved his ability to function well at home. Wife also expresses confidence that resident will do well and that she will be able to cope with any problems. Resident did well at home. He and family have overcome most of their fears and now feel they can cope with problems that may arise."

It may have been a little too soon for that record entry to be true in its entirety. Amy was still fearful. But she readily admits that adaptation to having Andy home, even with her working, occurred more easily than she had anticipated.

F·I·F·T·E·E·N

EARLY DAYS AT HOME

Once Andy got home,
he got more sure of himself.
He had to take care of himself,
so he did.

AMY ROBERTSON

Andy arrived home from Bay Pines quietly and without fanfare. Family and friends had grown used to him coming home for weekends, and this was another Friday. Amy pulled the car into the driveway beside their front door and helped him out. Sally was at work; she'd started a new job two months earlier. Susie was studying horticulture at a two-year technical college. Doug and Donald had gone on a weekend hunting trip. As Amy and Andy walked into the house, they were surprised to see a very tall philodendron plant winding around a stake on their patio. There was a card on it: "Welcome home Dad." It was signed by their sons. The plant stands on the patio today, and Andy proudly displays it to visitors.

The Robertson house, all on one floor, was ideally laid out for a recovering stroke victim. There is one step outside to the front door, one more inside from the family room to the patio. Otherwise, there are no built-in hindrances to walking, and the rooms are large, open, and easily accessible to one another. Andy's wheelchair had been left behind in favor of a cane, and no home therapy visits were necessary. The only physical changes Amy made in their surroundings were to have support bars installed beside the toilet, to add a tub stool for Andy to sit on while showering, and to push their twin beds together for his greater safety.

Andy was barely home, however, when Amy had reason to doubt the wisdom of his discharge from the Medical Center. He appeared to have lost all motivation. "He was like an invalid," Amy says. "He did his own bathing and things like that, but he hadn't really had to do anything for himself in so long that he didn't try now. He could get around, but we waited on him completely."

The swimming pool, at least, seemed to present no hazard. Andy had used it frequently before his stroke, but now he made no attempt to go near it. He says he simply had lost interest in it. Also, to get to it he'd have to go down that one step from the family room to the patio, and the step frightened him. He made no attempt even to go out on the patio.

The household routine, however, precluded babying Andy for long. If they were to make it financially, Amy had to continue working, and the Robertson children were either working or otherwise unavailable during the day. So, despite her fears, Amy started her day by preparing Andy's lunch and leaving it for him before she drove off to work.

Those first days were particularly difficult. She left her telephone number by the phone so he could call her if he wanted, and she wrote down her name because reading it aloud would be easier for him than simply trying to say it. Andy called frequently. Not only did that reassure her of his safety, but she was happy to learn that he could follow instructions, could dial the phone, and could make himself understood to the department store operator well enough to be put through to her.

Andy's mother also telephoned him every afternoon to make sure he was all right and to check on his needs. As the days passed, all of them began to gain the confidence they needed, Andy included. His fearful, tentative attitude began to soften as he grew accustomed to the daily routine. The transition from nursing home to home was going so smoothly that Amy had difficulty believing it and remembers little of it even today. "It was leaving him alone that made him do things," she says, "like get a glass of water when he was thirsty, get his own lunch—sometimes instead of preparing it, I'd leave something that would be easy for him to fix—and keep himself busy all day. He did it on his own beautifully. Now I'm sure he could have done it a lot sooner."

One problem that did come home with Andy, however, was the fits of crying. At first, he didn't have many visitors because Andy would burst into tears when they arrived and again when they were ready to leave. To give him time to develop more emotional control, Amy asked most of their friends to hold off for a while; she later regretted that because visitors seemed afraid to come. "It would have been better for the people to come and to let him cry," she says. "Then he would get over it. Instead it wasn't until he finally started getting out in the yard that he began to see neighbors." The fits of crying eventually passed, but Andy's emotions continue to remain close to the surface, and thoughts of old friends like Ed Moore prompt a few tears.

The Robertsons were living on Amy's pay now plus Andy's service pension, and Amy was careful to see to it that they lived within their means. Fortunately, Amy says, they were never much for credit-card spending. Fortunately also, because everything in the house had been so new when they moved in, there were very few replacement costs.

Once a week, Amy drove Andy back to Bay Pines for speech therapy. "Yes" and "no" were still his mainstays, but, with effort, a lot of other words were added, especially when he was talking to Amy or someone else close to him. They were one-word or two-word sentences, to be sure, but Andy was communicating. He was also able to communicate his wishes with clearly spoken expressions such as "Coffee, please" or "Water, please" and was able to bid his visitors "Good-by." Gradually, he added names and other nouns to his vocabulary.

Andy's biggest frustration was over his inability to drive. "If he could do one thing," Amy says, "that's what he'd want to do." Andy agrees, but indicates also that he has put the idea of driving out of his head. Part of resolving that problem came with professional counseling. Amy went with him to a psychologist at Bay Pines, and she recalls the discussion: "The psychologist told him that driving makes a man feel masculine, and that he doesn't need driving to feel masculine. He assured Andy that he was still a man even if he could no longer operate a car, and he helped him to deal with his feelings."

Amy was pleased with the outcome of the counseling from a practical point of view as well. Since she needed her car to get back and forth to work, Andy's driving would have meant the need for a second car—and one that was specially equipped for a man with a disabled right arm and leg. It was an expense she felt they could do without.

While inability to drive was the most difficult problem for Andy to overcome, the most difficult for Amy to deal with was the change in his temperament; he was like a new person to her, and she and the children had to get used to him. "I was so optimistic," she says. "I thought surely he was going to come around and be the same as he was. By the time we realized he wasn't, we'd gotten used to him as he was now, and we learned to live with it."

What they learned to live with were Andy's fits of temper, but his changed temperament did take its toll on his relations with the children. "They never really have been able to cope with his personality change," Amy says. "He flies off the handle so easily that they aren't comfortable with him. You have to be on your guard all the time, and young people don't have that type of patience. They don't answer him back, they just walk away, especially Doug, the oldest. He really takes it personally, and it hurts him. Fortunately, they understand. But it keeps them from getting really close."

Andy agrees that he no longer exhibits the sense of humor with his children that he did in the past, and he regrets his outbursts and their effect on family relations. He struggles to exercise more control but finds it difficult. So when his children find him angry, they have learned to keep their distance.

An entry in Andy's post-discharge medical record at the VA facility takes note of his problem: "Patience is short. Gratification must be instant. Has limited channels to use his energy. The genesis of these problems lies in his CVA (cerebrovascular accident or stroke)." According to another entry: "Showed early frustration when unable to accomplish because of physical handicaps."

Amy didn't just "learn to live with" Andy's fits of frustration. Over the year that he had been hospitalized, her independence and self-reliance had grown considerably. Still not an aggressive person, she nevertheless had lost some of her passivity. "I know I'm also harder to live with now," she says. "If I want to do something, I want to do it my way, and I don't let anybody push me around. So I'm not very easy to get along with either."

In addition to the weekly speech sessions, Amy also took Andy back to Bay Pines every three months for a checkup. The VA paid for the outpatient care, and, when special tests requiring fasting were required, even provided them with breakfast. But if, as sometimes happened, the VA personnel forgot to give them the breakfast chits, Amy could never bring herself to ask for them.

By all signs, Andy's recovery at home was progressing well. Then on July 6, Amy's wildest fears were realized. She was awakened in the middle of the night by a terrible shaking. Andy's legs shook, his body shook. She turned on the light to see him better and then rushed out of the room, calling Doug. "I really didn't know what to do for Andy," she says. "I tried to talk to him, to calm him. I let him know we were there. But the shaking continued." Meanwhile, Doug had immediately telephoned the local emergency squad and the medics sped to the house. Andy was almost over his attack when they arrived, but he had lost control of his bladder and bowels. The medics recommended that they immediately drive him back to the VA Medical Center in the ambulance, and Amy concurred.

Andy had suffered a seizure, a problem often afflicting stroke patients well into their recovery when scar tissue forms in the damaged portion of the brain. The fortunate aspect of his attack was that it occurred at a time when Amy was home rather than when she was at work. For the next two weeks, she felt as though she had stepped back in time, back to her routine of getting off work, grabbing a hamburger on the run, and visiting Andy in the hospital. He quickly grew impatient with the hospital stay and was very unhappy at being away from home again. "They would have kept him there longer," Amy says, "but he was ready to walk home from there if he had to. I was embarrassed, but I told the doctors he wanted to go home." Amy was confident now that they could manage alone at home, and the seizure had not recurred. So the hospital released Andy to her, and she once again drove him home from Bay Pines.

Four weeks later, at 5:30 a.m., Andy suffered a second attack, this one very short. Again Amy was roused from sleep, and again the emergency squad was called to the house. But this time, after Andy had recovered at home, Amy decided against having him taken back to the hospital. She made the same decision when he suffered another mild seizure in October, some weeks later. In December, when he had his fourth attack, she handled his care herself and didn't even call for help.

Andy's fifth attack, more than a year after his homecoming, was a major incident. He and Amy were in the kitchen preparing dinner when Andy suddenly got wobbly. Before Amy could reach him, he staggered backward across the room, reeling toward the kitchen counter. Then he fell, striking his head on the counter as he went down. Blood gushed from his head as he lay sprawled on the kitchen floor. Amy called the emergency squad and then helped him until the medics arrived. They put him in the ambulance and rushed him to the emergency room at the VA Medical Center once more. It took seven stitches to close his head wound. He also suffered a concussion.

This time a doctor at the hospital prescribed an antiseizure medication, Dilantin. It made the difference. That seizure was the last Andy has experienced to date; he still takes the medication once each morning and doubles that dosage at night. The only other medication he takes regularly is aspirin, which, in recent years, has gained more medical attention as a blood-thinning, antistroke medicine. He also takes vitamins as prescribed by his physicians at the Medical Center.

The trials didn't end. Andy started to put on weight. He was at 186 pounds when he was first admitted to the VA Medical Center, but, Amy says, "He goes overboard. If I didn't watch him, he'd weigh about 300 pounds. He doesn't realize how much he is eating, so he needs someone to clamp down on him." Outpatient physicians at the Medical Center now referred him to a dietitian, who put him on a strict, salt-free diet—under Amy's watchful eye.

He also was given exercises so that his disabled arm wouldn't atrophy from lack of use. "But he never had the motivation to do them," Amy says. "You see a lot of stroke patients whose arms have atrophied, and they warned him that his would, too, if he didn't exercise it. So far it hasn't, but it's hard to get him to do the exercises."

About this time Andy also went back for a visit to Dr. Romson, his family physician. No one can explain exactly what motivated the visit, since Andy was now under the care of the Medical Center. "I guess," Romson says, "he just wanted to see me." Whatever Andy's reason, Romson found great progress from the evening he had seen Andy in the emergency room at Morton Plant Hospital. Andy still couldn't use his right arm, but with a brace on his leg and the help of a crutch, Andy Robertson was mobile.

In part, what helped Andy's recovery was his own spirit. He always felt he was making progress. In large part, his recovery was due to Amy, her care and attention. But Amy says: "I think Andy is so independent *because* he was left alone while I was working. When men who have had strokes have their wives home with them all day, waiting on them, I think the men get very dependent. That's not good for them. Andy was afraid at first, but then he got more confident. If he had been left at the nursing home, I think he would still need to be taken care of. Taking him home was the right thing to do. He has done very well for what he has to deal with."

S·I·X·T·E·E·N

SEX
QUESTIONS
AND
ANSWERS

*I think sex is one of the
activities of daily living,
and anyone who leaves it out
is guilty of negligence.*

DOROTHEA D. GLASS, M.D.
Senior consultant
Moss Rehabilitation Hospital
Philadelphia

S exual counseling may be one of the most overlooked areas of rehabilitation, not only of the stroke patient but, equally important, of his spouse or partner. For one thing, the number of trained sex counselors skilled in dealing with the problems of the disabled is minimal. For another, there is a natural reluctance the patient and spouse may feel for initiating discussion of sexual matters and probably an almost equal reluctance by many health professionals to respond to them. In many institutions—probably it would be safe to say most—there is no formal sex counseling program for stroke patients. Even in the VA Medical Center at Bay Pines, where Andy Robertson's treatment was exemplary, a formal sex counseling program is only presently getting under way.

Resolving sexual problems and questions has been mostly a hit-or-miss matter. Sex as a subject has been often passed over lightly. If a spouse or patient raised a question with a health professional, that therapist, physician, or nurse might answer it perfunctorily or might refer the questioner to a more appropriate source for an answer. Discussions on this basis could hardly be expected to be extensive, and it is likely that some patients and spouses, having mustered up the courage to ask the question of one professional, did not follow through if they were referred to another. This sheepishness of patients and spouses, coupled with the laxity on the part of health professionals—who received little if any training in this area—argued the need for formal sex counseling programs that could bring the problems out in the open where they could be dealt with.

Still other factors tend to rob stroke victims and their spouses or partners of needed sex counseling. Perhaps the foremost is what we might call "the age factor." Because many stroke patients are "older"—sixties, seventies, and beyond—many times health professionals ignore the whole subject of sex. After all, they reason, "older people aren't interested in sex." Says rehabilitation nurse Menousek: "Therapists in such instances don't respond to elderly patients as sexual beings. We're just beginning to acknowledge that because you are old and have a sexual disability or handicap, that doesn't mean you have to give up sex." Those who provide sex counseling of the elderly disabled today, she says, are still in the forefront of this change in attitude.

The lack of sex-counseling training alone on the part of the health professionals has been a formidable obstacle to be overcome; it contributes to discomfort in therapist and patient alike. In recent years, though, Menousek notes, the number of workshops on sexuality has grown and professionals are getting better training in schools on the subject of dealing with patients' sexual concerns.

Certainly Amy and Andy Robertson had questions, but at that time, 1977, they received almost no sexual counseling. They did visit a psychologist at the VA—because of Andy's frustration at not being able to drive a car—but the issue of sexuality, Amy says, "just didn't come up." Nor is Amy Robertson the type of person who could have initiated a discussion about sex-after-stroke. At no time that she and Andy can recall were they ever counseled together about sex.

Amy was fortunate in one regard. One of Andy's key physicians at the VA Medical Center sat her down for about an hour one day and discussed with her the many aspects of Andy's condition. Within the scope of that discussion, he mentioned that they could resume sexual activity at the appropriate time. The physician, however, was foreign-born and spoke with a heavy accent, so Amy feels she missed much of what he was telling her. Again, it was not in her nature to interrupt and ask for clarifications. As she remembers her exposure to sexual counseling, "he said a couple of sentences about sex, and that was all we got."

On the strength of his comments, however, Amy and Andy felt safe in resuming their sexual activity on Andy's first visit home, five months after Andy's stroke and subsequent hospitalizations. Andy acknowledges that he initially felt less appealing to Amy because of his physical disabilities, a problem common to many stroke patients. But Amy felt no aversion to him and helped him push those feelings aside. "Sex was just natural," she says, "the same as it always was." Because of Andy's right-side limitations, some change in positioning was required, but there was no alteration in Andy's ability to achieve erection and perform sexually.

Both Andy and Amy agree that they had a satisfactory sex life before the stroke, and they feel it has not changed appreciably since the stroke. Rather than dimming Andy's enthusiasm for sex, for instance, stroke seems to have enhanced it to the point where the Robertsons are more sexually active now than they were before the stroke occurred.

Things are not exactly the same, however. Amy confesses to a declining interest in sex, which she attributes to the natural factor of aging. "I'm getting older," she says, "and it has hit me sooner than him. I'm just not as interested in sex." Also, perhaps peripherally related to the matter of sex, she feels some loss of the companionship she and Andy shared before his stroke because of her own busy schedule as the family breadwinner. "It doesn't seem as though I'm home much," she says, "and when I'm home I'm always busy trying to do housework or errands or something else. It doesn't seem like we are together much."

Undoubtedly the changes that occur both in stroke patients and their spouses and in their household life as well have a bearing on their sexual activity. So, too, do those many questions that may lurk in their minds and the feelings that provoked the questions. Dr. Dorothea D. Glass is experienced in dealing with such matters. She is a senior consultant and former medical director of Moss Rehabilitation Hospital in Philadelphia, a 150-bed hospital that deals with all major disabilities. She is also chairman emeritus and professor of the Department of Rehabilitation Medicine at Temple University School of Medicine. Here are her answers to some of the major questions about sex that concern stroke patients and their spouses:

When can sex resume after a stroke? "As soon as the patient's symptoms are stable enough so that the physicians and others taking care of him are not concerned about the state of his health. And the sooner it resumes, the better. For the most part, the problems that people experience sexually after a stroke are not necessarily organic. They're chiefly psychological, due to such things as changes in body image, depression—which is a normal reaction to a catastrophe like a stroke—fear or anxiety about the effects of active sex on the possibility of another stroke or on the patient's health, and how the stroke patient sees himself or herself and is seen by the spouse or partner."

Is sexual activity likely to cause a second stroke? "Having a stroke during sexual activity, especially during orgasm, is a very common fear of both partners. We know there is an elevation of blood pressure that accompanies sexual activity, but several studies indicate that it's no greater than the elevations that accompany normal daily activities. So anyone who can go through normal daily activities is generally safe having sex. I think sex is one of the activities of daily living, and it should be dealt with just the way you take care of dressing or grooming or eating. Any health professional who leaves it out is guilty of negligence."

Does age have any bearing on the resumption of sex? "Sexual activity in the healthy aged who have partners goes on almost to the last breath. Age is no contraindication. It's important that the elderly understand that there will be physical changes that normally come with age. A man will be slower to have an erection, and a woman will have a thinning of the vaginal mucosa and reduced lubrication. But those are things that can be dealt with just as everything else can."

Is sexual dysfunction a common problem of stroke? "No, it's usually not concomitant. Interestingly, though, a number of good studies that have been done show a considerable decrease in sexual activity. But they do not show anywhere near the same decrease in desire. In one study of 102 persons, there was about a 60 percent decrease in sexual activity but only a 14 percent decrease in desire. So even though there was a lot of depression, the desire was still there. Further, about 20 to 25 percent of couples report that they are more sexually active after the stroke than they were before. These may very well be the kind of persons for whom the sexual relationship was good enough before the stroke so that they never attempted to alter it. Now, for the first time, they take a look at themselves and say: 'We have some problems. What can we do to make sex better for us?' I know from our work with disabled persons at the rehabilitation hospital that the process of talking with your partner about your sexual life and how to improve it, including experimentation, generally makes sex better. I think that accounts for some of the increase in activity."

Are there physical disabilities that preclude sex? "There *are* physical problems, some more severe than others, but they don't necessarily preclude sex; they require sexual adjustments. Those may be hard for some people to make because people have all kinds of prejudices about what sexual positions are acceptable and what aren't. A stroke victim may suffer, for instance, from homonymous hemianopia—one side of his visual field is cut out. If that happens, and it's not uncommon, the partner has to be aware of it and see to it that when sexual activities take place, they can be directed to the side where the affected partner sees them.

"If the stroke has affected speech, then there will be a communication problem, and communication is a very important part of a good sexual relationship. If the aphasic patient can understand, however, the couple can develop their own language or communication system. Where receptive aphasia is involved, communication becomes very, very difficult. Mental impairment in general often leads spouses to feel that 'this is not the person I was in love with and married,' and that's a whole area that calls for counseling.

"Rarely, but sometimes—particularly in the left hemiplegic—there can be a loss of memory for sexual activity. The patient's whole knowledge of sexual activity may have been wiped out. You have to start all over again.

"There can also be mechanical problems due to paralysis or spasticity, but, in general, there are ways to compensate for anatomic problems. The partners need to be educated."

Are there specific contraindications to sex? "I would regard sex cautiously if it involves a recent hemorrhagic stroke victim. Heart disease, too, must be taken into consideration. It isn't that these people are ruled out from having sex, but that they might have to rely on alternative methods of sexual activity that don't require a great deal of energy. I get such patients started on caressing, pleasuring, in a recumbent position. It really doesn't require any more energy than lying in bed. In seeing patients on their admission to Moss Rehabilitation Hospital, we ask about their sexual adjustment as part of their medical history. That does several things: It indicates our belief that sex is one of the activities of daily living and is to be considered along with everything else, and it opens the door to discussion because patients are usually reluctant to bring the subject up themselves. They shouldn't be! They have a right to their sexuality, and they have a right to have their health professionals answer their questions. Certainly before their first visit home or their discharge from the hospital, someone should sit down with them and talk to them about specifics."

Do the drugs a patient takes after stroke affect him sexually? "Many of the antihypertensive drugs have a depressive effect on the libido as well as on sexual response and ejaculation. But the effect is variable; you almost have to see what it's going to be by trial and error. Dosages can be altered by the physician, but drugs, diabetes, and possible obstructive arteriosclerosis all have to be considered. They may inhibit sex, but they are not contraindications to sex."

How important is a good sex life to overall rehabilitation? "It improves rehabilitation tremendously. Some interesting studies of working-age stroke patients show that there is a distinct relationship between being successful sexually and being successful in resuming work. The two are intermingled. Similarly, someone who is vocationally rehabilitated and returns to work may suddenly start to become more sexually active. I'm referring to men and to the concept of impotence. It's hard to think of a man who is potent sexually as not being potent in terms of his ability to work. It's also hard to think of a man who's performing adequately at work as being sexually impotent. Lack of sexual activity adds tremendously to the pressure on recovering stroke patients."

Is there decreased touch sensation in the affected partner? "There is some loss of sensation to about half the body lengthwise, but the other half will have sensation left. Usually, the loss of sensation does not extend to the genitalia—but it may; it can be a problem especially for women patients. There may also, very rarely, be an absolute loss, temporarily or permanently, of a man's ability to have an erection or a woman's ability to lubricate. We're not aware of any reason anatomically why this should happen. However, the systems in the brain that control the autonomic nervous system, which is the system that governs response, can be affected. There is a tremendous amount of compensation, though. What we might call the sexual system is, in nature, a very protected system, and when one part of it is wiped out, other parts take over. Keep in mind, too, that, as indicated earlier, those who have strokes also often have diabetes or arteriosclerosis, which may affect some of the large vessels supplying the genitalia. These diseases could also be the reason behind a lack of response."

Is fear of being unattractive a common problem of stroke patients? "It is one of the most common, and it's very important that the partner understand it because the treatment for it is for the partner to become more straightforward, more expressive, to demonstrate that even though some things have changed, the other person is still loved and is still lovable and desirable. This can sometimes be very difficult, such as when a massive stroke causes a considerable personality change. A severe personality change rarely happens after a stroke, but there may be a temporary change, which can become fixed. The stroke patient has changed so the partner responds differently so the stroke patient then responds differently, and so on, back and forth. To deal with this problem, the partner has to understand that once the changes in the affected spouse stabilize, he will very likely return to his former self."

Suppose the unaffected spouse feels an aversion to the disabled body of the stroke patient? "She may indeed feel an aversion, and those who are caring for and counseling the patient need to be aware of her feelings and not put a burden of guilt on her. This is all very new to her, and it can be dealt with the way we deal with aversion generally—it requires that she have someone to talk her feelings out with. We find this problem with all kinds of disabilities, even very simple ones. First I try to find out if the spouse's attitude is really something new. Some spouses may have never really liked sex much to start with, and now they have an excuse not to participate. Or they may be put off by superstition, taboos, or myths, which abound in connection with the disabled. In history, there has been the superstition that disability is really a punishment for secret sins. Or there may be guilt attached to having sex with a disabled person. Once I find out what the specific problem is, I try to help the unaffected partner by accenting the positive, such as by leading her to think of the attractive things about her mate."

Doesn't a stroke patient's childlike dependence on his partner cause some reluctance on her part to have sexual relations with him? "Unless a person has suffered an unusually massive stroke, there's no reason for such complete dependence. That's just bad rehabilitation. One of the important things for patients, their partners, and health professionals to understand is that stroke is a condition from which you can be very well rehabilitated."

Not all doctors would agree with that. "It isn't that they wouldn't agree, they just don't know. I've had years and years of experience with stroke patients, and, unless there are complications such as loss of speech and understanding, a great deal of rehabilitation can be accomplished."

How much divorce have you seen after stroke? "I don't regard divorce as a major problem. Certainly the marriage that has been marginal is going to suffer as a result of the added stress put on it. There are also couples, however, who have been brought closer together by stroke. Some women have been waiting all their lives to have their husbands a little more dependent on them, someone to fuss over. Although others may want out of the situation, these can settle happily into it."

What specific advice would you give a couple who is re-approaching a sexual relationship? "Be aggressive about getting information on how to exercise your sexuality!"

As Dr. Glass indicates so strongly in the preceding questions and answers, sex is too important an aspect of a stroke couple's life to be buried under fears and inhibitions, all because of a lack of information. One place to start getting that information is from your family physician. If he can't answer your questions—or is uncomfortable dealing with them—he may be able to refer you to a psychologist or other counselor who can. The therapists you may deal with at a hospital or rehabilitation center are another possible source of information. So are the spouse support groups and, through the speakers on their programs, perhaps the local stroke club.

There are several more sources to contact for qualified professional help:

The American Association of Sex Educators, Counselors, and Therapists is headquartered at 11 Dupont Circle N.W., Suite 220, Washington, D.C. 20036 (202–462–1171). Its *National Register*, which was recently updated for 1984, lists professionals on a state-by-state basis according to their certification as sex educators, sex counselors, or sex therapists. Canada is also included. Although the *Register* does not indicate which of these professionals are experienced in dealing with the disabled, it could give you a good start on locating counseling in your own area, which might then, in turn, lead you to the most appropriate counselor or therapist for you. Cost of a copy of the *Register* is $5, and the association will provide it by mail. The organization, whose membership is divided into seven regional areas, also holds an annual conference and symposia for health professionals.

The Coalition on Sexuality and Disability, with headquarters at 122 E. 23rd Street, New York, N.Y. 10010, is another organization with a national network of health professionals—doctors, nurses, therapists, and so on. The Coalition focuses its educational efforts on the sexual aspects of disability and answers inquiries from individuals regarding sexual counseling services available from its members. Like the Association of Sex Educators, Counselors, and Therapists, it may be useful to you in locating appropriate counseling in your home area.

The Coalition also sponsors educational day-long and evening programs in the New York City area for the disabled and for health professionals. The programs are held in health-related facilities accessible to wheelchair patients and are offered at minimal cost. Notification of upcoming programs is sent to any persons who ask to be placed on the organization's mailing list.

The American Psychological Association, at 1200 17th Street N.W., Washington, D.C. 20036, is another avenue of inquiry. It will refer you to the psychological association in your own state, which, in turn, can help you find an appropriate counselor in your area. Or you may be able to locate your state association directly—they're often based in state capitals—and eliminate the need to call the APA, which does not refer to counselors directly.

The American Psychiatric Association, at 1400 K Street N.W., Washington, D.C. 20005, operates along much the same lines as the American Psychological Association. While it will not refer you to a counselor directly, it will give you the information you need to get in touch with the psychiatric association in your state or region, and that body should be able to help you find a psychiatrist locally with whom you can discuss your sex questions or problems.

Don't overlook other stroke resources mentioned in other sections of this book. If you feel you could benefit from sex counseling, what's important is not how you find the appropriate counselor but that you *do* find him or her.

S·E·V·E·N·T·E·E·N
STROKE
CLUBS

*At stroke club meetings, Andy
walks around like a big cheese,
greeting everybody. He makes
himself at home. He is at home
when he's there.*

AMY ROBERTSON

A woman in her mid-fifties, dressed in slacks and blouse, sits alone in what appears to be a semi-darkened living room, her right arm cradled in her left in a posture typical of a right hemiplegic stroke victim. A man a good deal younger, perhaps in his early thirties, thin, bearded, dressed casually, enters the room and walks over to her. He puts a hand tenderly on her shoulder.

"Mom," he says, "would you like me to turn on the television? Or maybe the radio?"

"I don't think so," she says plaintively. "There's never much on anymore."

"Would you like to put your feet up?" he asks. "I'll get you a hassock."

"I don't know," she says, her voice whiney with self-pity. "I suppose."

He pulls a hassock from another chair and puts it under her legs, then carefully raises her stroke-damaged right leg to rest on it.

"Is that better, Mom?" he asks.

Before she can answer, there is a knock at their door. The son opens it and shows in another middle-aged woman, Helen, a longtime friend of his mother's.

"Hello, Mike," Helen says. "Hello, Ginny. How are you?"

"Oh, I guess I'm all right," Ginny says. "You know..." Her voice trails off, leaving Helen to form her own conclusions.

"I was just getting Mom comfortable," Mike says. "She doesn't want to watch TV right now, so we were just talking."

Helen nods understandingly. "What I stopped by about," she says, "is to see if you'd like to go to a church supper this Saturday with me, Ginny. All your friends will be there. I thought you'd enjoy it."

"Oh, no," the man interjects, "Mother isn't ready for that yet. She's doing fine here."

"That's right, Helen," Ginny says. "I'm not ready to go out yet. I wouldn't want everyone looking at me."

"Sure you're ready," Helen argues. "It's been three months since you got out of the hospital. I could pick you up right here and then bring you home again. It's just for a few hours, and your friends would love to see you. I know you'd enjoy it. There will even be a talk by a horticulturist— might get you started with your garden again."

"No," her son responds emphatically. "Mother isn't strong enough yet to do any gardening. She might hurt herself. Maybe someday. Besides, suppose you had a car accident?"

"Oh, come on, Mike," Helen says. "It's time your mother got out and saw some of her old friends. It's wonderful of you to take such good care of her, but she needs more than that. She needs to get out and start living again."

"I'd feel foolish going out with all those people," Ginny says. "Suppose I had to go to the bathroom. I couldn't manage it alone."

"Ginny," Helen says, "we're your friends. We love you. We'd make sure you'd be all right."

"If you had a car accident, I'd never forgive myself for letting her go," Mike says.

"I'd drive carefully," Helen says. "It's only a short trip. Besides, accidents can happen anyplace. A fire could start right here in the house."

"Not with me here to take care of her," Mike says. "We're doing fine the way we are."

Suddenly a woman's voice from a darkened portion of the room calls out: "No, she should get out! She shouldn't stay home all the time."

"That's right," a man agrees loudly. "You've got to let your mother go out, son."

About thirty men and women are sitting on the edges of their folding chairs as the conflict around Ginny unfolds. This scene is being played at a monthly meeting of the Naples, Florida, Stroke Club. Helen, Mike, and Ginny are volunteer actors who call themselves "Everyday People," members of a community education and advocacy group called the Naples Mental Health Association Role Players. They are helping their audience confront a painful problem common to those with stroke disabilities: re-entry to social life after stroke.

There are hundreds of such stroke clubs in towns and cities across the United States. Many are under the auspices of the American Heart Association; others are independent. Like this one, many are run by volunteers who work with stroke victims in a professional capacity—therapists, for instance—and then give their time on a personal basis. They arrange programs, recruit members to participate, to provide refreshments, invite representatives of other organizations for the disabled, and pursue the same goal: to help stroke victims and their spouses help themselves, partly through the meeting programs and partly by socializing with one another.

At this meeting, for instance, the moderator of the players, a trim, neatly dressed woman in tan blouse and dark skirt, walks to the center of the room and faces the onlookers while the trio of players falls silent.

"Well," she says to the audience, "does any of this sound familiar?" A murmur of laughter runs through the audience, and you know the players have struck home. She hesitates a moment, looks around dramatically: "Does anyone else have anything to say to Mike?"

The comments start coming from around the room. The audience wants to be heard, and they all agree with Helen—Mike is being overprotective, and Ginny is too timid about re-entering society.

"Give your mother a chance to breathe," one woman admonishes Mike. "You're smothering her."

"You've got to get out on your own," another woman tells Ginny. "Go see your friends. You can't stay cooped up in that house."

Mike and Ginny argue back, as though they really were mother and son, but the audience won't accept their excuses. Then the moderator turns the direction of the encounter back on the audience. "What do you think?" she asks a man sitting in a wheelchair. "Did you have trouble going out the first time?"

He looks down at his legs and then up at her again. "It was hard," he says. "Sure people will look at you. But when you realize they're not laughing or making fun of you and they're not pitying you, just looking out of curiosity, then you get over it."

"What about you?" she asks an elderly man sitting quietly with his spouse. He tries to speak but no words come. "He can talk fine now at home," his wife says, "but when he's out he gets nervous and sometimes the words don't come out so easily."

Her husband begins to force out a few words. No one rushes him or interrupts him or tries to supply words for which he is groping. His great effort is obvious, but suddenly the words begin to flow. He addresses them to Mike. "Suppose something happened to you, Mike," he says. "Then what would your mother do? She has to learn to take care of herself. I drive. All over. We take trips. We travel on planes."

You can see the audience's attention growing as he continues, almost hear some of the onlookers saying to themselves: "He drives? He takes trips? He travels on planes?" There is inspiration in his words, hope, not just from an "outsider"—a doctor, therapist, or family member—but from someone who has actually experienced stroke, as so many in the audience have.

"The airlines are very good," his wife continues. "If you let them know you're coming, they take care of you. They take very good care of handicapped persons." Many in the audience obviously didn't know that the airlines would help, would arrange special services for their travel.

Suzanne Bernfeld, an occupational therapist, is the 5-foot-or-so bundle of energy who makes everything come together for this stroke club. Everyone at the meeting knows her, calls her Suzanne, treats her like an old, admired friend. She welcomes members by name, helps them get seated, makes sure volunteers reach everyone with cookies and punch at the prescribed moment, oversees the program of the day and plans the new ones. Today it was the Role Players. Another day it is a teacher of a "dancercize" class who volunteers her time to put the group through stretching exercises, after some expected health warnings and waivers of immunity.

Community activities are announced at meetings, what therapy is available locally, the formation of a singing group to assist those with speech problems. A heart-shaped box with names and phone numbers in it is offered around so members can pick out a "buddy" for regular weekly or monthly phone calls just to chat and share experiences. Another invited guest describes services available through a program for senior citizens at no charge, round-trip transportation to a tri-county seniors' center where they can enjoy bingo or singing around a piano, "just lots of fun for everyone."

Genuine concern is expressed for other recovering stroke patients in the community who do not come to stroke club meetings. "For every stroker here," Suzanne tells the attendees, "I'd estimate that three more are sitting in their homes, unaware of the club or held back from participating for some reason. We've got to find a way of reaching them."

Members volunteer suggestions. Newspaper publicity, advises one. "I've noticed that the newspaper often has write-ups on local clubs."

"I'll be glad to call the paper," says another, "but who do I contact there?" Someone else suggests a name, and the willing caller jots it down. Spouses, family members, and friends play major roles in the activities at the meetings, but the stroke victims themselves also participate to the extent of their abilities.

Suzanne wonders if maybe the "buddy" system couldn't be expanded. "There are a lot of people on our list who never come to a meeting," she says. "Maybe we ought to have others who do attend the meetings call them and invite them."

Someone suggests going further—having a stroker and his spouse visit those on the list to show them how the stroker is coping with his handicap and to open the club to them.

For now, the matter is unresolved. A private-duty nurse who accompanies a woman stroker reads a calendar of community events she has compiled for the club members—everything from church suppers to plays scheduled by a community theater. Two members receive cupcakes, each cake with a lighted candle in it, and are serenaded with a chorus of "Happy Birthday." Plans for a holiday party are announced, for luncheons, and for other club events, including the next meeting on the second Tuesday of the following month. The need for items about club members for a statewide bimonthly stroke clubs newsletter published by a state stroke council is reported. Suzanne reads the treasurer's report and reminds the group that there is new stroke literature on a table in the front of the room and that it is available without charge.

Stroke clubs like this are an aspect of care that can easily be overlooked during the acute stage of stroke and in the early stages of recovery. But they take on growing significance to their members as life-after-stroke proceeds. In addition to being a place where strokers don't feel "different," they are a place of learning.

"You don't know how to take your shoe off yourself?" a visiting occupational therapist asks an extremely well groomed elderly woman at a meeting. "Didn't you learn that in occupational therapy?"

"I didn't have any occupational therapy," the woman replies. "My doctor told me after six months that I was as good as I was ever going to be, and there was no sense in my throwing away money."

The therapist shakes her head. "Some doctors!" she says. She kneels beside the woman and begins to show her how to manipulate her legs to remove the shoe from the affected limb.

Andy Robertson is proud that, with all his therapy, it was a fellow stroke victim at a club meeting who taught him how to tie his shoes with one hand. He often demonstrates the technique to other strokers.

Andy's club meets the second Wednesday of each month, and in the four years since he and Amy joined it, they have missed only one meeting—in 1982 while they were away on vacation. "He just loves it," Amy says, "and I do too."

Andy was asked several times to become president of the club, but because his speech is so limited he has declined. He did not decline the office of treasurer, however, when it was offered about two years after he began his membership. "He balances the books," Amy says, "but he usually won't read the report, so I am the assistant treasurer. I stand up and give the report. Andy has it all written out very neatly on a big card, and he holds it up for everyone in the room to see."

It was during his second year as treasurer that his fellow strokers began to put pressure on him to take a greater role in the presentation of the report—an oral presentation. They recruited Amy's support, and it was en route to one of the meetings that she told him, "You're going to read the report today."

A newspaper columnist happened to be attending the meeting that day as a guest speaker, but Amy and Andy were unaware of his presence. Amy read the details of the report when it was called for, then stopped and called on Andy to announce the total the group had in its account. Andy rose to his feet as the other strokers waited. "Two hundred one dollars and eighty-six cents," he said. The club members cheered and applauded, not, the columnist was to write later, because the amount was so impressive but because it was the first time their treasurer had reported at a meeting. Andy proudly keeps that column among his mementos and shares it with visitors when the subject arises, written testimony to a significant achievement in his post-stroke recovery.

Andy and Amy had heard of stroke clubs through another stroke victim and through Morton Plant Hospital, but the nearest one is 16 miles away. "We meant to go," Amy says, "but we kept putting it off. Then one of the strokers called us and we finally went." Now it's their favorite activity.

"The people are just great," Amy says. "We have picnics and parties and interesting speakers, and we've learned quite a few things there. Andy is the youngest man there, and the other men and women act like our fathers and mothers. Everyone is interested in one another. One woman took us under her wing for the first few meetings and made us feel at home."

The club also gave the Robertsons something else—two special friends. "We've become very close to a couple who live in that area," Amy says. "After a meeting, we go out to dinner with them and then we go over to their home and play cards. Andy enjoys pinochle and gin rummy. The other man has a bit more speech than Andy, but he's not as easy to understand. What Andy says, he says very distinctly. But the two men have become very attached to each other."

The distance to club meetings and Amy's job present some impediments to further socializing with their new friends during the month. These factors also keep Amy from a separate support group for spouses, which she'd like to attend and which is a feature of the stroke programs at many hospitals. "The only day they could get for spouse support meetings at a local hospital was the day after the stroke club meeting," she says. "I couldn't take off two days in a row to attend. I wish we could work it out so it would be more convenient for me."

Her employment, however, does have advantages in terms of her overall availability for other things. "I just about make my own hours," she says, "so I take the second Wednesday off every month for stroke club meetings. If I worked at a bank or an insurance company, for example, I'd be working 9:00 to 5:00 every weekday, and I can't do that and do all the other things too, not only the meetings but take Andy to the VA hospital for checkups and so on. The job is ideal for that."

In her own quiet way, Amy has also become an on-the-job recruiter for stroke clubs. "When I wait on customers," she says, "I can tell immediately if they've had a stroke. I tell them about Andy, and I tell them how I'd like them to go to a strokers' club meeting."

Stroke clubs aren't for everyone, Amy cautions. "One man we met won't come to the meetings anymore because there are too many people and because there is too much talking. That's what the clubs are, though—people getting together and talking about their problems and learning from each other's mistakes or from what others are accomplishing. You have to be social to appreciate them, and Andy is very social. He walks around like a big cheese, greeting everybody. He feels so important when we're there. He just makes himself at home. He *is* at home when he's there."

A number of stroke clubs publish newsletters or provide news of members and other information in their monthly mailers announcing club meetings. It was in one such newsletter, published by Stroke Groups of Houston, that a doctor wrote: "Frequently, it is difficult for the stroke victim to recognize empathy in others. However, stroke victims do understand and accept it from fellow stroke victims. This may be the true reason for the success of stroke groups."

To locate a stroke club or stroke group near you, you would probably do well to contact your local hospital, therapists in your community, or the American Heart Association or its affiliate in your area.

E·I·G·H·T·E·E·N

LIFE
AFTER
STROKE

*Andy has come back
a long, long way.*

AMY ROBERTSON

Undeniably, stroke changes lives. Undeniably also, life-after-stroke can be far better than would seem possible on that first traumatic day when the stroke patient is rushed to the hospital.

For the Robertson family, life has changed appreciably since that dark, chilly morning when their ordeal began. Sally and Amy became so close through the months of Andy's hospitalization that, says Amy, "we even think alike now." Sally continues to live at home with her parents and now holds a more challenging job.

Doug has his real estate sales license and is also employed in a lumber business, in a way continuing family tradition. He had the shell of a house built for him on property he bought near a small lake about 40 miles from his parents' home, and he and his brother, Donald, finished the interior of the house themselves.

Donald graduated from college. About four years ago, the Robertsons gathered for his wedding, and pictures of the event caught Andy beaming happily and proudly as he walked down the church aisle, a cane his only means of support. Donald also did not move far from his parents' home.

Susie, the youngest, recently moved back home from her apartment about two miles away. She completed the two-year program in horticulture and has progressed from owning her own lawn-care business to owning a nursery while also holding down another job.

Amy's ailing mother passed away. Andy was with Amy when they got the news, and he handled it very well.

Amy continues to work full-time and has adjusted to her more demanding role in the household. Andy has adjusted to staying home and continues to make progress in a number of areas. Though he may use a cane when he goes out, he walks unaided throughout the house, a brace on his right leg. He keeps his weight down with Amy's help, no longer smokes, does household chores, paints well in acrylic with his left hand, travels alone on buses, and, twice, has passed a written test to renew his real estate broker's license—though his difficulty in communicating makes further such employment unlikely. He has also put behind him any thoughts of driving a car, though he occasionally backs the family car out of the driveway or pulls it into the garage while Amy stands by on pins and needles.

Other than his quarterly checkups, Andy has no therapy now. His outpatient speech therapy ended two years after his discharge from the Medical Center at Bay Pines. He has progressed from fearful to confident to aggressive, and he puts no limit on his own abilities. Should he drop his cane while walking in public, he declines the aid of passersby and insists on picking it up himself. Should a passerby drop something, he'll pick it up and return it. "He is independent," Amy says. "He wants to do things himself, and he doesn't want to be treated differently."

Sometimes he pushes himself beyond what Amy considers sensible limits. "I work almost 5 miles from home," she says, "and a few summers ago he was so anxious to see me about something that he walked over there in the heat. He was red-faced when he got there, and I told him not to do it again. But about a year later, he did it again." The food store nearest their home is about a mile distant, and Andy also makes that walk alone on occasion.

"It seems as though this is our normal life now," Amy says, "because we've been doing it for so long. It could be a lot worse."

If there is one thing more that Andy would like to be able to do today, it's talk. As noted previously, he can say many words individually and can even put two and sometimes three of them together occasionally. But fluency seems beyond him. Still, communication between Amy and Andy is generally not a problem. "Somehow," Amy says, "he usually manages to communicate with me. Sometimes it takes a while, and he'll have to write down a couple of words. Then I can usually get it. When I can't, it's like playing a game. I ask questions and make a few guesses. He may get impatient or upset, but usually we break through."

Sometimes, however, Andy's temper tantrums aren't so easily overcome. "The kids are a little timid about him," Amy says. "They see him slamming doors and things like that, and they're a bit standoffish. It's not their fault. They're just afraid of offending him and arousing his anger. So they don't always do as much for him as they might otherwise."

Has Andy's personality changed appreciably? Most of those who knew him before his stroke see little difference, but then their contacts with him are far less frequent than those of his family. Amy finds he has changed significantly. "This is a brand-new person," she says, "and there isn't much about him that is the same. I had to get to know him all over again."

Amy notes that prior to his stroke, Andy was very outgoing, very active, and liked to do things quickly. Now, she says, he's more reserved, less inclined to humor with the children, and loses his temper frequently. "He can't understand it when people can't do things the minute he wants them done," she says, "and he loses his temper. He never did that before."

Amy recently became sterner in her warnings to Andy, and that change in her attitude has somewhat toned down his explosiveness. Door-slamming episodes have, at least temporarily, ended. But Amy is also understanding. "I can't blame him for losing control," she says, "because that's typical of stroke persons. They get upset very easily. But I have to handle him with kid gloves."

The result, as might be expected, is that Amy must also cope with her own periods of frustration and depression. "Sometimes I get so angry when he gets upset that it takes me a day to cool off," she says. "I have to sleep on it or go to work or something. Actually, it's a good thing I'm working because I can be very upset when I leave in the morning, but I'll be at work fifteen minutes and I'll get over it. I'll forget it. So working is good therapy for me. But I'll be glad when I can just work part-time."

Her long-time employment in the same place provides Amy with an informal support group to help her over the rough spots. "Nearly all the people I've worked with for a long time have had a serious problem," she says, "either lost a husband or had a tragedy with one of their children or something like that. We all feel like a family, and we care for each other. If I weren't working, I would miss those people. We've gotten that close."

Andy, too, goes through times of depression, and to cope with them Amy reminds him of how far he's come from the day when he was first brought home in a wheelchair for a visit. "He couldn't do anything then," she says. "If he had to go to the bathroom, we had to push him there in the wheelchair. He just stayed in the chair or the bed because he was so weak. When he really gets down, I get him to think back on that—or even back further, to when he first had the stroke and couldn't point to his ears or nose or mouth. That usually helps."

Despite the problems and the frustrations, Amy says she does not get discouraged on any long-term basis. "I knew what I had to do and I did it. The Lord gave me the strength. I didn't pray all the time, but I knew that people were praying for me because I was never a strong person before but I always found the strength now to get through."

Although Amy assumed the role of family decision-maker when Andy was hospitalized and continues to run the household, she does share the day-to-day problems with him—whether they involve finances, a mechanical problem with the car, trouble with the plumbing, or whatever. He contributes to her decision as much as possible, but she also frequently calls Doug and Donald for help and advice. She has replaced her old car with a new one, but, prior to that, she says, "I was always calling on Doug for help when I had car trouble."

Not that she has ever reached the point where she finds the decision-making easy. "Lots of times I do the wrong thing, make the wrong decision," she says. "I change my mind a lot." At first Amy was reluctant to trust Andy with various responsibilities, but new roles for each of them have gradually emerged.

Before Andy came home, for instance, Amy handled the bill-paying among her other responsibilities. Now Andy has taken over that duty. "He used to make such a mess of the checkbook that I always had to step in and make sure the mortgage and the other bills were paid on time," she says. "Now as soon as we get a bill, he writes a check and I sign it. Then he waits a few days until it's appropriate to mail it. Our payments are never late."

What's more, Andy balances the checking account to the penny, using a calculator. "Before his stroke, it never balanced, and we were always overdrawn," Amy says. "Now it's always perfect."

Handling the checkbook is only one of the many chores Andy has taken over in the house—and taken over to Amy's satisfaction. From the day he left the VA Medical Center, he *expected* to make further progress at home— and his growing list of accomplishments attests to that progress.

That one step down to the patio, for instance, bothered him. For about a year after he came home, Andy avoided it. "All of a sudden, with great difficulty, he started getting down that step so he could get out on the patio," Amy says. "Now he does it every day. Carrying a basket of wet clothes, using just one arm and no cane, he'll walk down the step, past the pool, out the door, and across the grass—which a lot of strokers can't walk on because it unbalances them. Then with only the use of that left arm, he'll hang all the laundry out on the line for me."

The laundry is another of the household activities that Andy has assumed. Most days Andy is up before eight o'clock, while Amy is still sleeping. He'll go out to the kitchen, peel a banana, put it on the cutting board, and slice half of it, leaving the other half for Amy. Then he'll fix himself a bowl of cold cereal and banana, pour his juice, make instant coffee, or, more recently, make coffee in their new automatic coffee machine, and have breakfast.

It takes Andy about an hour to perform his morning ablutions, and some of this personal hygiene requires Amy's help. Washing his hair is the most difficult of these activities, along with washing his left arm, because he has not regained any use of his right arm. He shaves himself, using an electric razor or a safety razor held in his left hand. "It takes him a long time, and he can't do it if the razor isn't very sharp, but he always gets himself as neat as a pin," Amy says.

Afterward, with Amy off to work, he's alone in the house—except for two new dogs, Dixie and Rebel, that his daughters brought home several years ago as puppies. If the laundry basket is full, he'll find his written instructions near it from Amy: how to wash socks, sheets, underwear. By following the written instructions, he'll put the clothes in, set the dials, and do the wash. Then, even though they have a clothes-dryer, he'll follow Amy's preference and hang the wash to dry on the line in the yard. When the wash is dry, he'll bring it in, fold each item, and put it away.

"Not only does he do the laundry," Amy says, "but I never have to make beds anymore. He can do the dishes now, too. He even waits on me at times." Recently Andy expanded his duties to cleaning the kitchen counter, the bathroom mirror, and other items in the house. "He has developed such strength in his left hand that he can do almost as much with it as he could do with his right," Amy says. "I tried to hang the clothes out one day using just my left arm and hand, and it's very hard. You have to hold whatever you're hanging and open the clothespin with the same hand. It takes perseverance. You can't make it without that."

Next lesson for Andy on Amy's list is to teach him how to use their microwave oven. Meanwhile, he uses the stove. "He knows how to bake a potato, and, when I'm working late, he'll put a frozen dinner in the oven and bake his dinner and bake a potato with it," Amy says. "He can cook a hot dog, and he can use a can opener with one hand—it scares me, but he does it anyway. So he can always open a can of something and heat it. He also makes sandwiches and coffee, all, of course, using just his left hand."

Although Andy spends most of his days at home alone, he makes it a point not to pass the day watching television. Football, however, is another matter. He's an avid fan and can't get enough of the televised games.

Andy also takes phone messages during the day for Amy. His writing with his left hand has become firm and strong, and, though he can't write sentences, he can write down a name and address, a time and place, a phone number, and so on. Then he can use his notes to communicate his fuller message. He also likes to write notes to Amy, some personal and endearing as on their anniversaries, others simply indicating some things he wants done or wants to do. He enjoys looking up words in the dictionary and often copies their definitions.

Amy's concerns about the swimming pool have proved unfounded. While Andy enjoyed the pool before his stroke, he showed little interest in it for years afterward. In fact, he and Amy can recall only two instances of Andy using the pool in the years since his stroke. That may change. On a recent visit to the home of a stroke club member, Andy showed great interest in the hand rails his fellow stroker had installed going down the steps of his pool. The rails gave him easy access and made it easy for him to come out of the pool without assistance.

Part of the reason he hasn't used his own pool, Andy says, is that he found it so difficult to get in and out. He responded enthusiastically when Amy suggested they have the hand rails installed, and that addition should soon have Andy exercising again.

Twice a week, on trash pickup day, Andy carries the trash cans out and then puts them away later when they're empty. He's also gotten into the habit of putting away the trash cans for the two neighbors alongside them. When the neighbors are away on a trip, he also picks up their mail and newspapers for them. "He likes to do anything to get out of the house," Amy says. "Even if I was just going to the mail box, he'd want to come with me."

Togetherness to that extent also can cause Amy some frustrations. She'd like to be able to go shopping alone more often, but Andy wants to accompany her wherever she goes. "He also wants me to drive his way, park his way, and he ends up being upset by the way I do things. I can't get through to him that I'm not as good a driver as he was, that I can't just buzz out in front of traffic like he could. I have to take my time. Then in a store, if I stop to think about one item too long, he gets impatient. I tell him to sit down on a bench and watch the little children running around and the women."

Andy readily admits that he wants to be with Amy more now than he did before his stroke. Their togetherness problem has been alleviated partially by their discovery of the public bus system in their area, which gives Andy the opportunity to go out without always having to depend on Amy. "The buses are wonderful," Amy says. "They gave him independence."

She discovered the bus system in the area pretty much by accident. Andy had developed an interest in painting and drawing, a pastime he'd shown some talent for in his high school days. Amy found scenes in newspapers and magazines for him to copy, and both were amazed at how good his paintings were. "I couldn't believe it," Amy says proudly. "He's quite artistic, and it started coming out in him." But art classes for the handicapped were afternoon sessions held in a town some distance away, and Amy wasn't available to drive him there. "We'd been wanting him to go to that art class for a long time," she says, "but there seemed to be no way for him to get there. Then one day at a shopping center I saw a bus with the name of that town on it. I looked into the bus system and got all the schedules, and I found a bus he could take there."

For a time after his enrollment, Andy could take one bus a good part of the distance and then be picked up by car for the last part of the trip by someone in the program. When the availability of that car ride ended, it became necessary for him to transfer to a second bus—and his first such outing could have been his last if Andy had not regained his confidence. He transferred to the wrong bus. When he became aware of it, he realized also that he was riding through a familiar section of town—near his old real estate office—so he got off the bus and went to visit his friend and former business associate, Marv Chester, instead. Chester was delighted to see him, and they spent the afternoon driving around to different properties and socializing—an experience that they've repeated a number of times since. As a result, an experience that might have panicked some disabled persons turned out to be especially enjoyable for Andy.

The following week, he was on the bus again, made the correct transfer, and was back in art class. "It isn't just the art lesson he likes," Amy says. "It's being with the other people there who like to paint. I think they contribute a large part to his enjoyment."

Amy's investigation of the bus system also led her to research county services. While she found that most were limited to those aged fifty-five and over, she was able to get a special parking permit for their car and a card that enabled Andy to use the buses at half the regular fare because of his disability.

For a while, Andy took a bus to the Bay Pines Veterans Administration Medical Center to work as a volunteer, pushing wheelchair patients to their destinations in the hospital or rehabilitation unit. Then he abruptly stopped, with no explanation. A note in his medical progress record at the Center, however, indicates that he became disenchanted with the activity, perhaps because it was too difficult a cognitive problem at that time.

Andy's ability to use the bus has contributed to their social activities as well. Andy loves to dine out, so, once a week, he walks half a mile to a bus station and takes a bus to the mall where Amy works. He goes to a movie that starts at 2:00 p.m. in a theater there, and then meets Amy for dinner at 4:00. After dinner, he goes to a 5:00 p.m. movie while she returns to work. The movies cost only a dollar each, and both pictures are changed weekly. "We really do quite a few things," Amy says, "things that are conservative and don't cost a great deal of money."

Almost every evening, after dinner at home, they go to visit Amy's widowed father. Sometimes, tired from work, Amy would prefer to spend the evening at home, but Andy is always ready to go. They get home from the visit about 9:00 p.m., usually watch some television, and go to bed at 11:30, after watching the late news.

The television commercials also prompt episodes of "automatic language" on Andy's part. "He can get incensed at a commercial," Amy says, "and although he can't say many words, he can say the bad words. And he always says them. I guess there's no way he can stop saying them," she adds, "but afterwards, when I tell him what he said, he doesn't even realize he said it."

Because of such episodes, Amy was a bit wary when, in 1982, she and Andy were invited to spend two weeks vacationing with her sister and brother-in-law and a third couple at Cape Cod. Her sister had rented a cottage there and suggested that Amy and Andy visit. "I didn't want Andy embarrassing me with bad language or fits of temper," Amy says, "so I laid down the law to him. He was to behave himself, and, if he didn't, this would be the last time we'd go on vacation." Andy must have understood. They flew to the Cape and he behaved himself very well indeed. "He never exploded or slammed doors or anything like that," Amy says, "but once in a while, when something would go wrong, he'd use his favorite word. The others thought that was funny."

In fact, Amy says, Andy has done well on trips in general. Walt Disney World, in Orlando, Florida, is not far from their home, and she and Andy, accompanied by their two daughters, planned a weekend there. Because Amy felt it would be too much for Andy to spend the entire time on his feet, they rented a wheelchair and took turns pushing Andy around the grounds. "When we'd approach an attraction and the employees would see the wheelchair coming, they'd take us right in," Amy says. "We got to see almost everything because we didn't have to wait on lines."

They did run into one minor problem with a moving walkway, but the attendants overcame it. Nevertheless, the overall experience of pushing the chair throughout the day tired them to the point where they canceled their plans to stay a second day. "We all enjoyed it," Amy says, "but we were just too tired to do it again the next day."

Andy's sons have also taken him on camping trips. They bought a small trailer in which the three of them could sleep and have spent a number of weekends on a nearby game preserve.

Finances are still a concern for Amy and Andy, but their economic situation has improved considerably since the days immediately after Andy's stroke. His pension now amounts to $377 a month. In addition, Amy is earning between $13,000 and $14,000 a year, enough, with the pension, to carry them. "We're lucky that the children are old enough now to take care of themselves," Amy says.

She's careful, too, about their expenses. Such extravagances as long-distance phone calls, for example, are held to two a year—one each to Amy's brother and sister. The air-conditioner and major electrical appliances such as the clothes-dryer and the dishwasher are used infrequently. In fact, when something went wrong with the air-conditioner last year, the Robertsons let it go a year without being repaired. "Most of our neighbors are paying about $150 a month for air-conditioning," Amy says, "so I figured we saved that much." With part of that savings, she had ceiling fans installed in the bedrooms. The air-conditioner has since been repaired, but it's used very sparingly. As a result of their economies and income, they've been able to meet their $200-a-month mortgage payments, purchase the car outright for Amy, and put some money into savings, "just barely enough if we had a little trouble," she says. As one further economy measure, Amy has become Andy's barber.

Looking back, Amy finds that the stroke experience has made her aware of other victims. "I never used to notice how many people had suffered strokes until Andy had his," she says. "Now I can spot a stroke victim quickly, and I notice how common they are and how much damage strokes do."

As a result, she becomes angry with the impatience of others, particularly in public places, toward the disabled. "When Andy is walking in a public building, why don't people stand aside a bit and give him some room instead of always being in such a rush? Why don't schools teach children to stand aside or to offer help when they see someone with a cane?"

Often, her anger is also directed at the potential stroke victim. "It starts when I see a person who's overweight or who smokes," Amy says. "Doctors say that everything falls into place when your weight is down and your blood pressure is down. Why do people wait until it's too late? They have to be educated. When I see someone like that, I think: 'If only I could go up to you and tell you the whole story—while you still have time.'"

She thinks also of the kindness she and Andy have experienced, especially during the long term of his rehabilitation. "Regardless of who the patient was, or how old, or with what income, the therapists were patient and kind. At Bay Pines, they treated Andy as though he was their father, and, to me, to treat a stranger that way is the best you can do. They have done so much for him and received so little in return. We wouldn't have gotten along at all if it hadn't been for them. Andy has come back a long, long way."

She also expresses pleasure and pride in their children for their support through the ordeal of stroke. "The times we spend with our children now are the times I enjoy most," Amy says. "I really appreciate having all of them together. That's when I enjoy myself to the fullest. Our children are so good to us. All that counts is that we're all together. I had such a good time with them on my fiftieth birthday that I didn't even mind being fifty."

For the most part, Amy still takes life one day at a time, though she is also beginning to think of the future. Andy turned fifty-five in June 1984, and they eventually plan to take advantage of the tax exemption available to those fifty-five and older in the sale of their house. They'll buy a smaller one in the same area and put the financial difference between their sales price and their lower purchase price to work earning investment income for them. "Then maybe," Amy says cautiously, "I won't have to work so much in the years ahead. Maybe living will be a little bit easier. We hope."

APPENDIX

"One in ten American families is somehow touched by stroke."

That's the conclusion of the Denver-based National Stroke Association, newly formed under the leadership of Dr. Frank B. McGlone, a former president of the American Geriatrics Society. The Association, in which stroke victim/actress Patricia Neal is an honorary director, hopes to lessen the effects of stroke through public education and the exchange of information among stroke victims, their families, support groups, researchers, physicians, and rehabilitation specialists.

The Association will collect and catalog stroke-related materials and data, promote innovative models for support and rehabilitation of stroke victims, and make its collected data available to the public without charge by mail and by a toll-free information hotline to its clearinghouse. It will also provide referral to local stroke specialists and stroke support groups, encourage "networking" among stroke clubs, and, in short, "start a responsive information exchange system that unites all those involved with stroke into a powerful and national mutual support network." The hotline should be installed by the time you read this; the mailing address is 1420 Ogden Street, Denver, Colorado 80218.

Though the National Stroke Association is one of the newest forces on the stroke scene, it is by no means the only one. The National Easter Seal Society (2023 West Ogden Avenue, Chicago, Illinois 60612) may be the largest rehabilitation service in the nation. It has some nine hundred state and local chapters, provides services directly to patients or may refer them to other appropriate agencies in the community, and can provide equipment aids through local chapters.

The American Heart Association (7320 Greenville Avenue, Dallas, Texas 75231) has about two thousand state and local chapters or affiliates throughout the country. It provides stroke information and can refer stroke families to rehabilitation facilities in their local areas, stroke clubs, and other sources of help in their communities.

For those seeking help in occupational, physical, and/or speech therapy, there are also national associations that can refer you directly to sources of therapy or to local chapters familiar with the services and therapists available to you in your area. Their addresses:

American Occupational Therapy Association, 1383 Piccard Drive, Rockville, Maryland 20850

American Physical Therapy Association, 1156 15th Street N.W., Washington, D.C. 20005

American Speech-Language-Hearing Association, 10801 Rockville Pike, Rockville, Maryland 20852. The Association suggests that inquiries be directed to its consumer affiliate, the National Association for Hearing and Speech Action, at the same address. NAHSA will provide a list of certified speech-language pathologists by local area.

There are many other organizations, institutions, and agencies active in the stroke field. The Sister Kenny Institute (at 800 East 28th Street at Chicago Avenue, Minneapolis, Minnesota 55407) is one that provides outpatient and inpatient services as well as literature to stroke families. Moss Rehabilitation Hospital (at 12th Street and Tabor Road, Philadelphia, Pennsylvania 19141) is another. VA medical centers are open to those who meet eligibility requirements. Any university medical hospital is likely to have a stroke program. A recent survey conducted by the American Hospital Association also indicates that at least 70 rehabilitation hospitals are now in operation across the country and that about 345 hospitals have formalized rehabilitation units.

The point "formalized" is made because far more hospitals than that, in fact probably most hospitals, have some forms of rehabilitation available for stroke patients, whether that be physical, occupational, and/or speech therapy, but they may or may not have specifically designated rehabilitation beds. The government's new reimbursement procedures under Medicare, however, are likely to spur far more hospitals into establishing formal rehabilitation units.

It should interest stroke victims and spouses to know, too, that nearly half of all U.S. hospitals now have self-help programs for patients, also according to an American Hospital Association survey. While these programs are divided among patients with a wide range of illnesses, stroke support groups are among those found most frequently.

A wide variety of community resources are also available outside the hospital, and the hospital Social Services Department or a community social services worker can be a good source of referral to them. They include the local public health department, which might be able to supply a public health nurse as well as information on other agencies available; the Visiting Nurse Association; state vocational rehabilitation agencies; home health agencies; homemaker services; Meals-on-Wheels; stroke clubs, and even senior citizens' associations and church groups. A hospital auxiliary or the American Red Cross or another agency or the community itself may provide special transportation, such as Houston's curb-to-curb Metropolitan Transit

Authority service for the mentally and physically handicapped. Or, as in the case of Amy and Andy Robertson, a careful study of local bus stops and schedules may be all that's needed to help your stroke patient to achieve a greater degree of independence.

The stroke picture would not be complete without mentioning the efforts government is making in the field. Overall, federal institutes have funded hundreds of research projects aimed at stroke prevention, improved diagnostic techniques, and improved outcomes for patients. In fact, over the past two decades, in the words of the National Institutes of Health, "cerebrovascular disease has become a topic of intense research interest in some of the nation's best scientific institutions."

Several years ago, the National Institute of Neurological and Communicative Disorders and Stroke (NINCDS) established three regional comprehensive stroke centers—one at the University of Rochester, New York, another at the University of Oregon, and the third with the North Carolina Heart Association. These centers, according to the National Institutes of Health, serve as regional focal points for applied and community research, help evaluate local resources for patient care, and provide data so that research results can be transferred to the communities.

A national stroke data bank, funded by the NINCDS, has completed its first three-year pilot phase and is now into a five-year phase of data collection dealing with the study, treatment, and prevention of cerebrovascular disease.

The NINCDS also funds thirteen clinical cerebrovascular research centers at universities and medical centers across the country, including University of Alabama, Birmingham; Baylor College of Medicine, Houston, Texas; Bowman Gray School of Medicine in Winston-Salem, North Carolina; Cornell University Medical College, New York, New York; Duke University, Durham, North Carolina; University of Maryland, College Park; Massachusetts General Hospital, Boston; Mayo Medical School, Rochester, Minnesota; University of Miami, Miami, Florida; University of Oregon School of Medicine, Eugene; University of Pennsylvania, Philadelphia; Rush-Presbyterian-St. Luke's Medical Center, Chicago, Illinois; and Washington University, St. Louis, Missouri.

The NINCDS is active on other fronts as well. It has contributed many millions of dollars to research aimed both at the problems of cerebral circulation and metabolism and at the training of research scientists. In 1982, it completed a five-year international cooperative study of bypass operations within the brain. The bypass operation was found to be feasible, but whether it is more effective than medical care without surgery remains to be determined by long-term monitoring and evaluation of the patients studied.

Another federal institute attacking the problem of stroke is the National

Heart, Lung, and Blood Institute. Much of its research focuses on hypertension, atherosclerosis, and heart and vascular disease, all related, of course, to cerebrovascular disease. Programs it has sponsored have produced important information regarding the risk factors of stroke. The National High Blood Pressure Education Program was also coordinated by this institute.

"Since this program began," according to the NINCDS, "there has been a continual improvement in the public's knowledge about high blood pressure, an increase in patient visits for hypertension, and a substantial rise in the percentage of hypertensives who are aware of their condition and who are under treatment." At the same time, it notes, "We have witnessed a dramatic drop in stroke mortality"—a drop we hope will continue.

GLOSSARY

Though many of the terms used in this book are explained in the text, here are some terms commonly used by physicians as they apply to stroke.

Aneurysm	A sac, or pouch, in an artery wall, caused by the ballooning out of a weak spot in the wall.
Aphasia	Loss of the use and/or comprehension of spoken and/or written language.
Arteriosclerosis	A hardening or thickening of artery walls.
Artery	A blood vessel that carries blood away from the heart to the various parts of the body.
Atherosclerosis	Deposits of a fatty substance called plaque build up on the inner walls of arteries, narrowing the passageway so that the flow of blood through the artery is slowed.
Blood pressure	The pressure of the blood on artery walls as a result of the pumping motion of the heart. Diastolic pressure is the pressure when the heart is relaxed between strokes; systolic refers to the pressure when the heart beats.
Cerebral	Refers to the main portion of the brain.
Cerebral embolism	The blocking of a cerebral artery by a clot, called an embolus, that originated in an area away from the brain.
Cerebral hemorrhage	The bursting of an artery in the brain, causing blood to flow into brain tissue or the surrounding space.
Cerebral infarction	Death of brain tissue due to interrupted flow of blood through a brain artery.
Cerebral thrombosis	The blocking of a cerebral blood vessel or a vessel leading to the brain by a clot, called a thrombus, that originated in that brain or neck (carotid) artery.
Cerebrovascular	Refers to the blood vessels of the brain.
Cerebrovascular accident (CVA)	See *Stroke*.
Cerebrovascular occlusion	The closing off of a cerebral artery by a clot or a spasm.
Coagulation	The clotting of the blood.
Contractures	A permanent shortening of a muscle or tendon causing deformity; illustrated by the muscle's strong resistance to passive pressure.

Diplopia	Double vision.
Dysarthria	Poor articulation of words due to damage to the nervous system.
Dysphagia	Swallowing difficulty.
Dysphasia	An impairment—less severe than aphasia—in the ability to communicate by language.
Embolic infarction	The blocking of a cerebral artery by a clot, causing the death of brain tissue.
Embolism	The blocking of an artery by a clot, or embolus.
Embolus	A clot or plug carried through the circulatory system that eventually obstructs a small blood vessel.
Endarterectomy	The surgical removal of plaque from the inner walls of an artery.
Hemianopia	Blindness or another defect in vision affecting half the visual field.
Hemiparesis	A partial or mild paralysis or muscle weakness of one side of the body.
Hemiplegia	Paralysis of one side of the body.
Hemorrhage	Bleeding; uncontrolled flow of blood from the vessels.
Hemorrhagic stroke	A stroke, or CVA, caused by the bursting of a cerebral artery and the subsequent flow of blood into the brain or its surrounding area.
Hypertension	Blood pressure persistently higher than normal.
Infarction	Death of tissue, such as brain tissue, generally due to a restriction of blood flow.
Intracerebral hemorrhage	Bleeding within the brain.
Intraparenchymatous hemorrhage (IPH)	Spontaneous bleeding into the brain tissue; also referred to as parenchymatous hemorrhage.
Ischemia	Restriction of blood flow due to blockage of a blood vessel.
Left hemiplegia	Stroke damage to the right side of the brain, which leaves the left side of the body paralyzed. The left hemiplegic is likely to have difficulty relating to time and space, memory problems, and an impulsive behavior.
Little stroke	Temporary interruption of the blood flow to the brain, often experienced as dizziness or a feeling of confusion; also called transient ischemic attack (TIA). The effects pass within twenty-four hours.
Neural	Refers to a nerve or the nerves.
Nuchal rigidity	Stiffness of the nucha, or back of the neck.

Parenchymatous hemorrhage	See *Intraparenchymatous hemorrhage.*
Right hemiplegia	Damage to the left side of the brain, which results in paralysis to the right side of the body. The right hemiplegic is likely to suffer aphasia or dysphasia and to exhibit a slow, cautious behavior.
Ruptured aneurysm	A bursting of the aneurysm, or sac, in the weakened wall of the blood vessel, resulting in a hemorrhagic stroke.
Stenosis	The narrowing of an artery internally, restricting the flow of blood.
Stroke	Damage to the brain resulting from a disruption in the flow of blood through a cerebral artery; a cerebrovascular accident.
Subarachnoid hemorrhage	Bleeding into the (subarachnoid) space surrounding the brain.
Thrombotic infarction	The closing of a cerebral blood vessel by a clot, or thrombus, cutting off the flow of blood and causing the death of brain tissue.
Thrombus	A clot that forms in an artery and eventually obstructs the flow of blood through that vessel.
Transient ischemic attack (TIA)	A little, or small, stroke; a passing, temporary blood deficiency in a cerebral artery; see also *Little stroke.*
Vascular	Referring to the blood vessels.
Vascular occlusion	The closing off of a blood vessel.

INDEX

Dizziness, 19
Double vision, 14, 19
Driving, 136–137, 161
Dysarthria, 15
Dysphasia, 15, 41, 46

Edema, 11, 27
Effects of stroke, 41–48
Electroencephalogram, 16
Embolic stroke, 13, 14, 22, 27
Embolism, 13
Emergency room, 7–16, 27
Emotional control, loss of, 42–44, 82, 136, 137, 162
Exercise. *See* Physical therapy
Exercise, pre-stroke lack of, 21–22
Expenses, 37, 55, 56, 63, 75–78, 90–91, 136, 168–169
Expressive aphasia, 41

Facial paralysis, 15
Family, 13, 28–29, 55, 57–59, 81, 87–92; counseling, 98–99, 131–132, 143, 149–150, 171–173; involvement in rehabilitation therapy, 71, 98–100, 102–103, 106–107, 109; recovery guidelines for, 46–48; and stroke victim at home, 133–139, 161–169
Feeding, 38, 107
Friends, 63, 129–130
Frustration, 42, 126, 137, 165–166

Graphic skills, 69
Guidelines, recovery, 46–48
Guidelines for Stroke Care, 20–22, 29, 35, 58, 59, 114

Headache, 14, 19, 27
Health insurance, 5, 77
Heart disease, 22, 146
Hemiparesis, 15, 41
Hemiplegia, 15, 41

Hemorrhagic stroke, 11, 12–16, 27, 35, 30
High blood pressure, 11, 16, 20, 22, 23, 105, 174
Home health care and recovery, 5, 76, 77, 78, 98–99, 106–107, 109, 111–121, 133–139, 161–169; agencies, 113–115; exercises, 115–121
Hospital: discharge, 58, 106, 131–132; emergency room, 7–16, 27; expenses, 37, 55, 56, 63, 75–78; ICU, 16, 27–32, 36–38, 52; length of stay, 37, 38, 58; stroke team, 51–59; VA, 56, 63, 81–84, 87, 95–110, 125–132
Hygiene, 63–64, 67, 107, 108, 125, 126, 130

Infarction, 11–13, 41
Information sources, 149–150, 171–174
Initial stroke, 29, 30
Intensive care unit (ICU), 16, 27–32, 36–38, 52
Intermediate care facilities, 113
Intraparenchymatous hemorrhage (IPH), 14, 35
Ischemic stroke, 12–16, 35, 38
Isotopic brain scan, 16

Left hemiplegics, 15, 41, 44–48, 146
Leg exercises, 117–119
Lifestyle, pre-stroke, 19, 21–22

Medicaid, 76, 77
Medicare, 37, 75–76, 113, 114
Medication, 3 , 139, 146–147
Memory problems, 13, 43–46, 48, 67, 146
Men, 30, 35
Motivation for recovery, 57, 101, 103, 126, 130, 135, 139
Muscle therapy, 54, 100–104, 105–106, 125

National Heart, Lung, and Blood Institute, 22, 174
National Institute of Neurological and Communicative Disorders and Stroke, 9, 12, 173–174
National Survey on Stroke, 12, 14, 22–23, 29–30
Neal, Patricia, 14, 36, 171
Neurologist, 52
Nuclear brain scan, 11, 15
Numbness, 19
Nurses, 52–53, 97–100
Nursing homes, 110, 127–132

Obesity, 20
Occupational therapy, 54–55, 102, 107–109, 125
Oral contraceptives, 23
Oral encoding, 68
Outpatient care, 77, 78, 101, 137–138
Oxygen, 12

Pain, 27
Paralysis, 11, 13, 15, 38, 41–45, 97, 147
Paraphasic errors, 6
Parenchymatous hemorrhage, 14
Paresis, 13, 15
Perseveration, 67
Personality changes: post-stroke, 42–48, 125–126, 136, 137, 147–148, 162; as warning of stroke, 19
Physiatrist, 52
Physical therapy, 52, 53, 54, 64, 100–104, 125; home exercises, 115–121
Physician, 51–52, 56–57, 114
Plaque buildup, 13, 22
Pneumonia, 11, 37, 99
Positron emission tomography (PET), 15
Prevention, stroke, 35–36, 100, 103

Professional help: sources of, 149–150, 171–174; stroke team, 51–59
Progressive stroke, 15
Prosody, 69
Public transportation, 166–167, 173

Receptive aphasia, 41, 146
Recovery rate, 35–36
Recreational therapist, 56
Recurrent strokes, 31
Rehabilitation, 37, 38; corrective therapy, 56, 104–107; costs, 75–78; early stages, 41–48; family involvement in, 46–48, 71, 98–100, 102–103, 106–107, 109; occupational therapy, 54–55, 102, 107–109, 125; physical therapy, 54, 64, 100–104, 125; post-hospital, 75, 76, 77, 78, 98–99, 106–107, 109, 111–121, 133–139, 161–169; professional team for, 51–59; rehabilitation nursing, 53, 97–100; sexual, 143–150; speech and language therapy, 43–44, 47, 55–56, 64–72, 125, 136, 161
Rehabilitation hospital, 113
Religion, 92
Respiratory problems, 11, 37
Reversible ischemic neurological deficit (RIND), 21
Right hemiplegics, 15, 41–48, 54–55, 125
Risks, stroke, 19–23
Ruptured aneurysm, 12

Seizures, 14, 138–139
Self-confidence, 38, 130
Sensory deprivation, 41–42
Sequence planning, 69–70
Sex, 42, 143–150
Skilled nursing facilities, 113
Social Security, 76, 77

— 181 —

Social Service Department
 benefits, 75–78
Social worker, 55
Spatial disorientation, 38, 45, 46;
 therapy, 64–65
Speech and language therapy, 43–
 44, 47, 55–56, 64–72, 125,
 136, 161
Speech disorders, 11, 13, 15, 19,
 41–45, 64–72, 146, 162
Spinal tap, 11, 16
Spouse support groups, 57–58,
 77
Staff rehabilitation nurse, 97
State institutions, 113
Statistics, stroke, 29–31, 35
Stenosis, 23
Stiff neck, 14
Stress, 21
Stroke, defined, 12
Stroke clubs, 72, 153–158
Stupor, 14
Subarchnoid hemorrhage (SAH),
 14
Surgery, 27–28
Survival rate, 35–36
Swallowing, 38
Swelling, brain, 11, 27

Symptoms, 6–7, 14–15
Syntax, 68–69

Therapy. See Rehabilitation
Thrombosis, 14, 102
Thrombotic stroke, 13, 14, 21, 23
Tingling, 14
Transient ischemic attack (TIA),
 21, 22
Trigylcerides, 21
Type of stroke, 11–15

Ultrasound, 16
Urinary tract infection, 65, 99

VA hospitals, 56, 63, 81–84, 87,
 95–110, 125–132
VA pension, 96, 128, 168
Vision, impaired, 14, 45, 146; as
 warning of stroke, 19–21
Visual perception, 67–68
Vomiting, 11, 14

Walking, 104, 105, 125, 129, 161
Warning signs of stroke, 19–23
Wheelchair, 54, 96, 125, 126,
 127, 129, 167–168
Women, 30, 35